Spiritual
Growth

Spiritual Growth was taught as a class to a group of people over the period of a year. One year after the course ended, class members got together to share with each other some of the changes they had experienced in their lives from using these techniques and following their paths of spiritual growth. We would like to share some of their comments with you about what spiritual growth has given them:

"More joy—unbelievable joy."

"I never feel alone anymore, nor am I afraid to be by myself."

"Freedom from expectations—it has improved all my relationships."

"Self-acceptance and a whole new level of self-love."

"I have realized I can let things come easily into my life without struggle."

"Serenity and a sense of wholeness."

"Passion—a passion for living!"

"I feel expansive and clear more frequently."

"Meaning and a sense of purpose."

"It has empowered me to be who I am and speak my truth."

"Fun—I am having more fun than ever before."

"A greater sense of oneness, more community and support from others."

"I realize now I've always been on a spiritual growth path but not conscious of it."

"I am never bored anymore!"

"Opportunities and more choices than ever before."

"I feel like I am finally coming home. Things make more sense, and I have answers to my questions."

"An increased sense of inner knowingness; the whispers are stronger."

"It has given me the courage to allow people to be who they are and empower them to move through their lessons, rather than try to take away their lessons."

"I no longer see my lessons and challenges as obstacles but as fuel that makes my growth faster and easier."

BOOK III EARTH LIFE SERIES

Spiritual Growth

BEING YOUR HIGHER SELF

Sanaya Roman
CHANNEL FOR ORIN

H J Kramer Inc
Tiburon, California

H J Kramer Inc
P.O. Box 1082
Tiburon, CA 94920

Library of Congress Cataloging in Publication Data

Roman, Sanaya.
    Spiritual growth.

    (Earth life series ; bk. 3)
    Bibliography: p.
    1. Spirit writings.   2. Spiritual life—Miscellanea.
I. Title.   II. Series: Roman, Sanaya. Earth life series ; bk. 3.
BFI301.R75 1989   133.9'3   88-81721
ISBN 0-915811-12-X (pbk.)

Cover art: "Harmonic Convergence" © 1987 by Judith Cornell
Cover design: Tony Van Diggelen
Book design and production: LaserGraphics, Oakland, CA

Manufactured in the United States of America
10 9 8 7 6 5 4 3 2 1

To our readers,

The books we publish are the contribution that we are making to an emerging world based on cooperation rather than on competition, on affirmation of the human spirit rather than on self-doubt, and on the certainty that all humanity is connected. Our goal is to touch as many lives as possible with a message of hope for a better world.

Hal and Linda Kramer
Publishers

To *your birth into light.*

Orin

ACKNOWLEDGMENTS

To Orin, whose love, guidance, and wisdom has empowered me in every aspect of my life and assisted me in connecting with my Higher Self.

I want to thank Duane Packer and his guide DaBen, who have added many treasures of love, understanding, and spiritual growth to my life. DaBen has spent hours and had countless dialogues with Orin refining philosophical issues and developing energy techniques. I send my deep gratitude to Duane for all the energy work he has done with me, teaching me how to achieve higher energy states, open my clairvoyant sight, and develop my body of light. I want to thank Duane for the many hours he spent with Orin and me, reading this book back to Orin, asking questions, and giving us valuable feedback. He and DaBen have added much light to this book and to my life.

This book came from transcripts of classes taught to a small group over the period of a year. The class members used these principles and had many wonderful results in their lives; their feedback was most valuable. I want to acknowledge those of you who assisted in holding a focus for the chapters in this book: Ed Alpern, Amerinda Alpern, Marianne Anderson, Mary Beth Braun, Rosemary Crane, Dona Crowder, Wendy Grace, Carol Hawkinson, Roberta Heath, Colleen Hicks, Sandy Hobson, Sylvia Larson, Trudie London, Mary Pat Mahan, Sara McJunkin, Nancy McJunkin, Patrice Noli, Jill O'Hara, Eva Rosa, Jan Shelley, and Leah Warren.

I wish to thank those who contributed to putting Orin's channelings into written form: Elaine Ratner, for her wonderful editing and suggestions, and Linda Merrill for her thoughtful editing assistance. I want to thank Hal and Linda Kramer for being so wonderful to work with, for the example they set of living in integrity, and for their encouragement and support of Orin's and DaBen's work. I want to thank Denise Laws for transcribing Orin's channelings and David Duty for his excellent book design. Lastly, I want to thank Judith Cornell for her outstanding cover artwork.

I want to thank Georgia Schroer for her loving service in managing the office and her willingness to grow.

I want to thank those of you who have added much light to my life: my nieces and nephews, John, Elise, Mary, Tabatha, Heather, and Justin; my parents, Court and Shirley Smith; my uncle, Otto Brown; Rob Roman; my brothers and sisters, Debra, Patricia, David, and Robert; and my wonderful friend, LaUna Huffines. Many thanks and much love to all our seminar assistants, including those already mentioned, who have added much light to our and others' lives: Sandy Chapin, Cindy Haupert, Judy Heckerman, Johanna Holmes, Rhonda Holt, Rikki Kirtzner, JoAnne Marsau, Tom Oliver, Nina Page, Shirley Runco, Phillip Weber, and Cheryle Winn.

I also thank a very special dog, Comet, and his owners, Sue, Rich, and Shannon, who shared him so generously, for his wonderful companionship and our longs walks together in Mount Shasta.

A very special thanks to the bookstores that carry new age books, for contributing to the awakening of people to their higher potential through this wonderful service, and for their support of Orin's and DaBen's work.

CONTENTS

PREFACE

Orin and I welcome you to this book, the third in the Earth Life series. You can read and use each book in the series individually; together they provide a course in higher consciousness.

I have been channeling Orin, a spiritual guide and teacher, for more than ten years. He tells us he is a being of light and is here because we are going through a time of major transition and awakening. He says he exists in the same dimension as our Higher Selves, and that part of his purpose is to assist us in being our Higher Selves in our earth lives.

I have always experienced Orin as a very wise and gentle being. His advice to me and others assists us in connecting with our Higher Selves and our own inner wisdom. When I channel Orin, I am in a peaceful state similar to meditation and am conscious of his guidance as it comes through me.

I perceive his guidance as a stream of thoughts alongside my own, and I am aware that we have two distinct streams of consciousness. I feel as if I am bathed in light when I channel; there is an incredible sense of love and understanding. Orin's words seem like a fraction of what I am experiencing; there is a richness of feeling, pictures, and illumination transmitted with his words that is beyond description.

You may feel this richness yourself as you read this book, for Orin tells us that he has designed these sentences so that their rhythm assists you to open your breathing and move into a

higher state of consciousness. In this state, you are more connected to your Higher Self and may receive pictures, feelings,
and inner-knowing that go beyond the information you are
reading. Orin reminds us to accept only the information that
rings true to the deepest part of our beings and set aside any
that does not.

The material in this book was originally taught by Orin to a
small class of students, to teach us more about spiritual growth,
accelerate our growth, and assist us in growing with joy rather
than struggle. Orin gave us information and taught us how to
get into higher states of consciousness through guided meditations, energy techniques, and breath work.

Since then, we have had many opportunities to use the
techniques given in this book. They have brought us many
positive results. We all feel we have taken a quantum leap in
our spiritual growth and have had wonderful changes in our
lives. As we have used these tools of the higher realms, we have
learned to create many things that would have seemed like
miracles before. Today we use these processes almost automatically, for they seem quite normal. We often take their
effectiveness for granted and forget that we once did things any
other way.

In the class, we called upon the power of light and changed
difficult situations for the better. We learned to become transparent and let others' energies pass through us. We received
wise counsel from our Higher Selves and found new ways of
handling old patterns. We saw the bigger picture of our lives
more clearly and learned new information about our higher
purposes and who we are. We discovered that spiritual growth
could be richly rewarding and more fun than we had thought.

Orin told us that the information covered in the class would
be the basis for this book, and that he was aware of each and
every one of you who would be reading it. In his reality there is
no time and space. As he talked to us, he made us aware that he
was also talking to you. He had us spend time during the
classes connecting with you, telling us to imagine lines of light

going from our hearts to yours, greeting you across time and space as our fellow classmates.

As Orin and I were organizing the class notes and putting this book together, he often had me stop and let him broadcast energy through me to you. I had a sense of an enormous amount of love pouring through me, and I knew when the energy left my body, going outward and making a connection to someone. Although I do not know which of you Orin is sending energy to, you will know who you are as you read this book and feel his love and support reaching out to you.

At other times while we were working on this book Orin had me send out love through my heart to all of you as a group. He had me imagine us as a loving, connected community of like-minded souls, assisting each other through our inner connection. He says that all of us who are growing and evolving are generating as a group an enormous amount of light that is becoming a profound source of awakening for others.

I am glad to share with you all the tools that Orin has given me to assist me in growing spiritually, discovering my higher path, and becoming a source of light. I have come to realize that spiritual growth is a wonderful journey, and I welcome you as a fellow traveler on the path. I send you light as I join you in the inner planes where we are all working together.

How to Use This Book

This is a course in spiritual growth. Section 1, Reaching Upward, is about becoming one with your Higher Self and connecting with the higher powers of the universe—the Universal Mind, Higher Will, and light as a living entity.

The second section, Opening Inward, is about creating oneness with all the parts of yourself through opening your heart. You can learn to love yourself more, allow even better things into your life, calm your emotions, live in the void, choose the reality you want, and change your experience of time.

In the third section, Expanding Outward, you will learn about creating oneness and unity with all life on your physical plane and becoming a source of light. You will have the opportunity to learn more about who you are, your higher purpose, and how to take your work out to the world and grow through service. Empowering others and shifting their consciousness will assist you in going even higher yourself.

Orin has designed the guided meditations that follow each chapter to take you through a step-by-step process of spiritual growth. As you do these guided meditations, sit quietly, read them, and use your imagination. Do them in as high and focused a state as you can. Notice when you feel a shift, for the meditations are designed to shift your energy higher. Pretend you are doing whatever the meditation calls for, and use the images, thoughts, or ideas that flow into your mind as guidance from your Higher Self. We have used certain pictures and symbols to lead you to special experiences. Use or change these pictures as you see fit to enhance your inner experience, for the feeling of the desired state is more important than the images we have used to lead you there.

As you read and use each meditation, you will be gaining tools to connect upward, evolve yourself, and become a source of light to others. You can do these processes mentally, have a friend read them to you, or put the processes on tape and play them back. For your convenience, Orin has made audio cassette meditation tapes of many of the topics covered in the book as well.

Orin and I send you our love as you become your Higher Self and open to your greater potential.

– Sanaya
(Pronounced Sah-nay-ah)

Introduction:
Earth Changes

Greetings From Orin!

You are entering a dramatic and exciting time. There is a wave of energy passing through your galaxy that is altering the course of all life it touches. This wave affects the very nature of energy and matter, bringing all matter into a higher vibration. Although it is just beginning to come to the earth plane, you may already be feeling the effects of this higher vibration of light. You may be receiving more insights, having more frequent psychic and telepathic experiences, and feeling a deeper need to know your life purpose and put it into action. You may feel you have less time and more to do, for this wave changes the nature of time.

Some of us have come as guides to assist you during this special time. We have discovered much about this wave of energy; we know that it is light and it is conscious. We have discovered that by working with and aligning with this light the potential for evolution and growth is enormous.

Your ancient prophets foretold this wave, and the thought of major transformation during your current time was seeded to prepare you for it. Some have foreseen it as a time of earth upheavals. Such upheavals need not occur; they are symbolic of the internal changes that may happen as thoughts, feelings, and attitudes of a lower nature leave and are replaced by those of a higher nature.

You can ride this wave of light and experience more joy, peace, and love than you have ever known. Begin to do so by embracing your spiritual growth, linking with your Higher Self, and working with light. Take small steps as they appear to you, grow in harmony with nature and the earth, and then you will be in alignment with the higher vibrations this wave brings.

You are building a body of light.

You are rapidly evolving into a new race of beings. Because of the new, massive influx of light, a body of light is evolving in the human aura. The beginning stages of this light body are built around the heart and slightly above the heart in the upper chest. Some of you get chest colds, congestion, or heart flutterings as your light body is being built in this area. The new wave of light is challenging you to open your heart and bring both your "energy" heart and physical heart into a higher vibration.

Your light body allows you to become a radiating source of light. Much as the earth generates its own magnetic field continuously, as you build your light body you will generate and radiate light and spiritual power that will assist you and others in going higher.

As you become more radiant you may become increasingly sensitive to food. You may already be feeling a desire to change your diet or gain a new level of physical fitness, for your body is directing you to those changes that will allow you to hold and radiate more light.

As you build your light body, your intellectual mind will still be strong, but it will blend more with your intuitive mind. You will find yourself drawn to those things that are creative and challenge you to reach into deeper levels of your being. You will have a growing bond and kinship with all life-forms. You can already see this happening in humanity's awakening consciousness of animal rights and the need to preserve wild-life and forests.

You are preparing to become a telepathic race, and part of your preparation is to become aware of many other realities. You are experiencing a constant flood of new information and input from many sources. This is assisting you in developing the quality of discernment as you decide what to accept as your truth. When you are completely open telepathically, you will want to have the ability to select what comes into your field of awareness, be able to stay in your center, and understand and detach from views and beliefs that aren't in harmony with yours.

You came here to build your body of light and transform matter into a higher vibration. You call this transformation "spiritual growth." As you grow you become your Higher Self, a being of light. As you grow you are bringing the high, fine energy of your Higher Self into matter and transforming the potential of consciousness in this dimension.

Many of you are very sensitive to energy.

Your sensitivity allows you to sense, direct, and work with the higher, finer energies that are coming. You volunteered to go first and to be on the leading edge of the wave as it moves through the earth plane, so you could find ways to grow and heal yourself and then assist others as they feel the wave's impact. You may have noticed that in the last few years you have had to grow rapidly, go through much transition, and learn many new things. As this wave of light becomes stronger, more and more people will be waking up to what you are already experiencing. As they do, you will have more and more opportunities to be a teacher and a source of light.

Wave upon wave of higher consciousness is coming. Each one will create an enormous group opening, followed by a period of integration while the wave recedes. Each wave of higher vibration will be bigger than the one before. Its effects will be more noticeable because the number of people able to experience it will increase. Among other things, these waves will increase your desire to focus on spiritual growth and to discover your higher purpose. These waves will assist you in discovering the higher dimensions of yourself and achieving higher states of consciousness.

As new waves first come they may be felt as turbulence; they may shake things up in your life so you can make changes that will allow you to go even higher. It will become easier to go upward and be your Higher Self as each shift occurs. As you align with your Higher Self, you will no longer feel turbulence as these waves come, but will be able to use their power to lift you higher and take you to your goals more rapidly.

Many people may reject these shifts in the beginning, for to incorporate them may mean a complete change in the way they perceive and live their lives. Some may feel they are unable to handle the higher energy, and may try to deaden its effects through alcohol or drugs. Some may try to hang on to the old and find that doing so is an increasing struggle. Some may resist by criticizing the new ways or reacting with skepticism and doubt. Some people have to experience a high level of struggle and pain before they pay attention to and follow the inner messages they are receiving. At any point they can decide to follow the inner messages they receive and grow through joy.

Not opening to and flowing with this higher vibration will have larger and larger consequences. If one area of your life is stuck, unhappy, or doesn't work, it will affect every other area of your life. It will no longer work to ignore those areas of your life you do not want to deal with. If you don't like your job, are having trouble with a relationship, or live in an unsupportive environment, that will dampen your aliveness in every other area.

This new wave of energy will have a great impact on those areas of your life that have the least clarity and harmony. This new wave adds light to your life, but you can hold light only in those places where there is clarity and harmony. You will find that the areas that aren't working become the most important to resolve and that doing so brings you the greatest growth.

Your alignment with this wave of light can assist humanity and the earth in making a calm, peaceful transition. The way you embrace the changes in your own life, seek out your growth, and let go easily of those things that no longer serve you will affect the course of humanity and the earth. The transition into this higher vibratory frequency can be made with love and joy rather than pain and upheaval.

Light is not yet distributed evenly over the planet; it is coming most strongly to those places you call "power spots." From those power spots the waves radiate outward in larger and larger circles of influence. Power spots exist all over the world, in every city and community. You can recognize them by your increased ability to go upward when you are on them. We see power spots making up an enormous gridwork of energy that is growing and able to influence more and more matter.

Although these new energies are increasing, they are still very subtle. For you who have finely tuned your awareness through channeling, meditation, and other self-awareness techniques, the energies are more noticeable.

In this wave of higher energy, you will find you need to nurture yourself and follow your inner prompting toward joyful activities from moment to moment. As you nurture yourself, your desire to reach out and make a contribution to others will increase. The new times that are coming will place more importance than in the past on community, family, and connections with loved ones. You may find yourself wanting to network and connect with others of like mind, for much will be accomplished by people working together. Humanity is becoming more inclusive and group-oriented.

You have already witnessed the beginnings of humanity's working together telepathically to create change in your global peace meditations. This collective effort by millions has already had a profound influence on the spiritual awakening of many people and is accelerating the spiritual transformation of humanity.

This higher vibration that is now coming to your planet is going to be even more compatible with you who are on a path of spiritual growth than anything you have experienced in the past. As you make the changes your inner messages suggest, your careers are going to take off, your plans are going to succeed, and you will get whatever you want that is for your higher good.

It is no longer a question of having what you want, but of making sure you want what you ask for—for you will get it. What you ask for will appear more and more rapidly, for the laws of manifestation are taking on aspects of the higher planes. In the higher dimensions, you experience what you think about immediately.

Never before have there been so many paths, so many possibilities, and the opportunity to choose what reality you want to experience. The most important aspect of these new energies is the opportunity they offer for joy, growth, and aliveness. They will help you awaken to the multidimensional being you are, tap into the greater plan of humanity's evolution, and discover the part you came to play in these wonderful, exciting times of transformation.

1

Being
Your Higher Self

As you grow spiritually, you are on a wonderful journey of self-discovery. You will increasingly understand the mysteries of the universe and learn tools of personal transformation. As you go higher, your life can be effortless. Everything you need will come to you as you need it and your creative endeavors will bring you results beyond anything you can imagine.

Spiritual growth is a journey as vast as consciousness. In this book I will give you some tools, information, and techniques to assist you in growing more easily and joyfully. This knowledge will assist you in getting to the next level, where your growth will come almost entirely from directly experiencing higher energy states and connecting with your Higher Self.

"Spiritual growth," as I will describe it, means growing through connecting with your Higher Self and to a Higher Power—the God/Goddess within and without, Christ, Allah, Buddha, the All-That-Is. This connection will bring you aliveness, a healthy body, loving friends, a supportive environment, and the opportunity to make a difference in the world.

The spiritual path can be one of immense play and deep inner joy.

Spiritual growth gives you the tools to make your everyday life work and bring increasingly higher levels of order, harmony, clarity, and love into every area of your life. Spiritual growth is the single most important thing you can focus on if you want a joyful, peaceful, and loving life.

As you grow spiritually you will be able to see the bigger picture of your life. As you link your will with the Higher Will, you will gain more awareness of the path of humanity's evolution and your part in it. You will discover your life's work and gain the tools to carry it out. Your life's work will make a meaningful contribution to people, the plant or animal kingdoms, or the earth itself. It will be something you love to do. You can do what you love all the time; your work can be your play.

As you open to the higher dimensions of yourself, you will be able to lift the veils of illusion and see the world through the eyes of your Higher Self. You will link your throat with your Higher Self and express truth and love in all you say. Your mind will be illumined and your emotions will be harmonious as they are blended with the light of your Higher Self.

Spiritual growth assists you in creating loving relationships. As you grow spiritually, you will connect with people in higher ways. Your growth will allow you to trust more, keep your heart open, and reach new levels of sharing and intimacy. You will have deeper, more meaningful connections with your loved ones.

What many of you are looking for in another—compassion, understanding, and love—you will find first in your connection to your Higher Self. This connection will enable you to love and nurture yourself more and to connect with others in higher, more loving ways.

Your Higher Self loves you unconditionally.

As you grow, you will know how to send light to strengthen and empower yourself and your friends. You will trust your ability to sense energy so much you will feel safe wherever you are. You will hear your inner guidance clearly and take action on it. You will easily harmonize with the energies of all kinds of people. You will learn how to become transparent to or even transmute "negative" energy. You will experience friendly smiles, love, and peace wherever you go.

At higher levels of consciousness you will become more aware of subtle energies. You will gain an ability to feel, sense, and even see the subtle vibrations of other dimensions, life-forms, and the auras that surround people's bodies. Your higher powers of clairvoyance, telepathy, and other psychic abilities will become enhanced, although they will be only tools to further your growth and not ends in themselves. You will be able to create rapid, positive changes in your physical body and gain greater skill in healing yourself.

Your fears may not be totally gone, but when a fear comes up you won't react with even more fear. Instead you will talk to the fear, send it love, and ask for any message it contains. You will notice immediately when you are not in a high state, and you will be able to get rapidly back to a balanced, centered, and calm state.

Spiritual growth is similar to personal growth, with one big difference: when you grow spiritually you are connecting with a higher power and using that connection to empower your growth. This higher power—your Higher Self and God/All-That-Is—works with your personality self, assisting it to develop self-confidence, self-love, clarity, and other important qualities. When you work on your personal growth and add to that your connection to a higher power, your journey is even more joyful, rapid, and transformative.

*There is no limit to the growth and expansion
that is possible for you.*

Enlightenment is being very skilled at holding and radiating light. Enlightenment is not a place you reach where you stop growing and are perfect. No matter how high you go there are higher and higher levels you can reach. Being enlightened means that you have tools and resources to handle all the energies about you in such a way that you add clarity, harmony, and light to everything around you. Energy is ever-changing and, as far as I and others in my dimensions can tell, there is no limit to the growth that is possible.

When you reach a certain level of radiance and light you may choose not to be born into another lifetime on earth, but instead to live in other dimensions that offer you different opportunities to become a more radiant being. Or, you may choose to come back, for as you grow you have the ability to make a greater and greater contribution and become even more radiant through your service to others.

There are many paths to enlightenment. Choose the path that is most joyful to you and in alignment with your values. You may choose one path at one time and another path at another time, or you may try several paths at the same time. Go toward those disciplines you are drawn to; don't feel you must pursue something that doesn't appeal to you just because others say it is the "right" way to grow. Each of you is unique. Trust your Higher Self to lead you to those processes that are most appropriate for you.

One of the first things you can do to grow spiritually is to let go of any preconceived ideas you have about spiritual growth and your current level of evolution. You may have heard that if you were spiritually evolved you would have memories of your past lives, be able to meditate for hours, live in states of continual bliss, and acquire superhuman abilities, such as being able to leave your body or live for hundreds of years. While some of these things may happen naturally during certain stages of your growth, it is not necessary to be able to do these things to be highly evolved.

Many highly evolved souls have no past-life memories and do not demonstrate superhuman abilities or spend their days meditating. You will find evolved souls working in every possible area to lift the condition of humanity, raise consciousness, and bring more light to their areas of service. They are doing many practical things with their lives and creating many positive results. Their work acts as their meditation and provides their opportunities for spiritual growth. They have learned to focus upward while they are focused outward in service. They do not need superhuman abilities to accomplish their higher purpose.

Spiritual growth is the process of becoming your Higher Self.

Your Higher Self is a dynamic, growing life-force consciousness. It exists in a realm where all beings are united as one multidimensional consciousness. Your everyday consciousness is an aspect of your Higher Self that lives in your physical reality. Your Higher Self sends you impulses to be loving and united with others. Your Higher Self knows harmony, order, and light; when you add these to your life you are operating as your Higher Self.

Your Higher Self knows why you have the challenges that you have. Your Higher Self is the very essence of who you are and holds the accumulated knowledge from all your lifetimes. It is the wise teacher that exists within you. Your Higher Self knows no limits and is not attached to any role you play. It can heal and evolve you as you bring its high, fine vibration into your body and all your energy systems.

Your Higher Self usually talks to you through your intuition and feelings. It can also communicate by sending you odd coincidences and synchronicity—in the forms of people, newspapers, books, movies, and anything else that will give you the messages you need to hear. As you strengthen your connection to your Higher Self you will experience increasing insights, revelations, and expanded awareness.

You can take an enormous leap forward in your spiritual growth by contacting your Higher Self. Some of you begin contact by imagining yourself talking to a wise teacher or advisor and asking for advice. We will be working with the next step, which is *being* your Higher Self. You will learn to directly experience the feelings, thoughts, and wisdom of your Higher Self and to be your Higher Self more and more often, until this is who you are all the time.

You can be your Higher Self at every moment. Your Higher Self is your expanded, loving, wise, and compassionate self. You already are your Higher Self at those moments you are focusing on what you are doing, coming from your heart, or receiving creative insights. You are your Higher Self as you work with light, shift consciousness in others, or focus on how you can serve and make a difference in the world. I will assist you in recognizing how it feels to live as your Higher Self and bring its greater light into every area of your life. As you recognize those instances when you are already being your Higher Self, you can bring them into your life more often.

Spiritual growth comes from increasing contact with your Higher Self and allowing It to become the director of every part of your life. Once you begin a path of spiritual growth—seeking, learning, exploring the greater being that you are, and uncovering the mysteries of the universe—you will never be the same. You may stop for a while or decide to slow down, but after you experience the joy of growing you will not want to stand still for long. As many of you are already aware, once you have embarked on this adventure of growth, you may never want to stop!

Being Your Higher Self

MEDITATION

The purpose of this meditation is for you to connect with that part of yourself that *is* your Higher Self, and feel your Higher Self as *you*.

For all the meditations, sit quietly, focus your mind, relax your body, and start by taking a deep breath. You may want to put on music that calms you and takes you higher. You can do the meditations by reading them to yourself, having a friend read them to you, or by tape-recording them and playing them back. You may want a pen and paper or a tape recorder to record your answers.

Steps:

1. Sit with your eyes open or closed. Adjust your posture so that you are comfortable, perhaps putting your hands at your sides. Begin by taking a few deep breaths.

2. Imagine your entire body relaxing, starting with your toes. Bring a feeling of relaxation into your feet, calves, and thighs, then up into your abdomen and lower back, chest, upper back, and shoulders. Next relax your arms, hands, neck, head, and face. Let the muscles around your jaws and eyes relax. Do this until you feel peaceful, focused, and physically comfortable.

3. Adjust your posture so that your energy can flow more easily up and down your spine. Breathe a full breath into just your upper chest, moving your lower diaphragm and abdomen as little as possible. Breathe into your upper

chest several times; notice how you feel. Now breathe into your abdomen several times, following this with several breaths into both your upper chest and abdomen.

4. Straighten and lift your upper chest with a deep breath, so your spine is more upright. Notice that as you do this you may also want to adjust the back of your head and neck to the most comfortable upright posture. This helps create fluidity in your emotional body, open your heart center, and make it easier to think in higher ways.

5. You are now ready to meet your Higher Self. Imagine that you are being joined by many high beings who are sitting in a circle around you. Feel the peace, joy, and love all around you. These beings are here to assist you in meeting your Higher Self.

6. Imagine your Higher Self in the distance, beginning to come toward you. You might picture It as a beautiful, shimmering, radiant light. Greet and welcome your Higher Self and invite It to come closer. Mentally ask your Higher Self to assist you in making a stronger connection. Feel the radiance of Its love surrounding you and embracing you. Feel the lines of light coming to you from your Higher Self. As these lines of light touch you, feel your vibration increase. Your Higher Self is now merging and becoming one with you. Feel your molecules and atoms merging with It, as if you are reclaiming a part of your energy. Let your Higher Self merge with you even more until all your energy patterns are taking on the radiance of your Higher Self. You and your Higher Self are now one.

7. As your Higher Self, open your breathing to create a greater flow of energy in your body. Adjust your posture so that you are sitting as your Higher Self. As your Higher

Self, adjust your shoulders and chest to reflect your confidence and wisdom. What facial expression do you have as your Higher Self?

8. Think of a situation you want guidance about. As your Higher Self, you are going to give yourself advice about this situation. Imagine you are a wise teacher and consultant. What advice would you give yourself on this situation? You may want to speak out loud or write down your answers.

9. As your Higher Self, do you have any other messages, perhaps about your spiritual growth, your higher purpose, or anything else?

10. Thank your Higher Self for becoming one with you and sit as long as you like as your Higher Self.

I will call this the "Higher Self" state. You may want to use the steps just described for those meditations that follow that say, "Get into your Higher Self state for this meditation." You will find that the more you practice this state the more you will want to think about your future and important decisions only when you are in this state. As you go into your Higher Self state, you gain the skill and ability necessary to live your life as your Higher Self.

2

Creating With Light

Light is one of the most powerful forces in the universe. You might think of light as a living presence that can be anywhere or everywhere at once. It responds to your thoughts of it. Light is present in all known universes, although not in exactly the same form as in yours.

Light is a potent force of transformation; that is why the new wave of light that is moving through your universe is creating so many changes. You can use light to strengthen your connection to your Higher Self. You can call upon it to transmute energy and to empower and heal yourself and your loved ones. Light can increase your vibration, amplify the strength of your positive thoughts, and open your heart. You can link with it, harness its power, and create good all around you.

The power of light
is growing stronger every day.

The amount of light on your planet is reaching critical mass; the forces of light are growing stronger every day. That means everything you do that is positive and loving is more influential than anything you do that is not. It was not always this way. In the distant past, the power of light on your planet wasn't as great. It took a great deal of intent and focus to create something good. It took a lot of work to shift energy to a higher order. As the forces of light continue to grow stronger, even a small step toward your higher good and spiritual growth will take you further faster than at any time in the past.

Your intuitive understanding of what light is and how to connect with it is more important than any definitions I could give you. If I were to say to you, "Connect with the light," you would instinctively know how to do that, for your Higher Self is always connected with light. As you think of light you begin to vibrate with your Higher Self.

You can bring more light into your life by thinking of it. Light responds to your thought of it; as you think of it, it is immediately drawn to you. At first it is easier to draw light to you than it is to radiate light. As you think of light more often, you will become charged with light, building a radiant body of light all around you. The more light your body can hold, the higher your vibration and the greater your ability to transform the energy around you into a higher order.

Stop for a moment and call light to yourself.

Imagine you are standing under a waterfall of sparkling light, and that your body and aura are becoming more and more radiant. Feel light flowing through your body. Just thinking of light will rejuvenate your body at a cellular level and increase your available energy. Light can lift you to your next level of growth and dramatically change what you experience.

Connect with light for a few moments during the day—at work, in your car, at home, or in a store. Every time you connect with light you are building a bridge between yourself and the higher realms. As you build this bridge of light you will become more radiant and effective on the earth plane in whatever you are doing.

A very powerful use of light is to imagine that you are putting up a sphere or cocoon of light around you, which extends above your head and below your feet. I have included an energy meditation at the end of this chapter to assist you in doing this. Do not think of light as a protection, but as an energy that is so strong it raises the vibration of everything around you. Use this image to create within you a feeling of strength, harmony, and love. When you surround yourself with light you do not have to build a wall around you to keep things out; your light will transform everything around you into a higher vibration.

You raise your vibration when you surround yourself with the image of light. Your higher energy will set a tone that others around you can pick up. Not everyone is capable of responding to your higher vibration, but as you put light around yourself, you make a higher vibration available to others. You will be more able to stay calm and centered, and will find it easier to keep your heart open and be compassionate and loving.

If you are at a business meeting or social gathering where little is getting accomplished, or you want to change what is happening, sit quietly and call in light. Imagine light all around you, and extend it to encircle all the people present. You will notice subtle and sometimes not so subtle changes. Keep thinking of light and increase your own sense of inner peace, harmony, and love. One woman was in a very trying courtroom situation, defending herself against a lawsuit she felt was unjust. She put light all around herself for several days in a row, and was amazed to watch the atmosphere change and become more supportive of her cause. The final judgment was in her favor.

As you call in light, you may notice your heart opening more and more. It will be easier to feel more trust in the universe and know that nothing can hurt you. You will gain the confidence that comes from being able to create good things in your life and knowing you are in charge of your destiny. Light can aid you in feeling peaceful no matter what is going on around you.

Sending light can create harmony in your relationships.

If you feel separated from someone you love for any reason, you can change the energy between you by working with light. For instance, if someone is upset with you, you might normally work hard to calm that person. Instead, get quiet and call light to you, charging yourself with as much light as you can. Make your own energy as beautiful as you can imagine it to be. Then, send light from your heart to the other person's heart. Keep doing this, and sooner or later you will notice a positive shift in the feeling between you.

One woman's husband tried to control her by yelling and getting angry when she didn't do what he wanted. She always tried hard to please him, but her efforts seemed only to make things worse. One day, during an argument, an idea came to her. Rather than fighting, she withdrew to another room and imagined her energy to be as beautiful and clear as possible. She surrounded herself with light, and soon felt herself grow more peaceful.

She began to send her husband peaceful, loving thoughts, but made no physical move to calm him. She sent light to him. A little while later, he came in to talk to her as if the argument had never taken place. That was the fastest they had ever recovered from a fight, and all she did was calm down, make her own energy beautiful, and radiate light to him. In the past, her physical and verbal efforts to calm him down had only made things worse.

There are many practical ways you can use light. When you are traveling, you may want to put light around yourself and the vehicle you are in so you feel safe and protected. You may also want to put light around your home when you leave. As your children or loved ones go off to school or leave home each day, put light around them. Your loving thoughts and images of light will be with them throughout the day, serving to keep them safe and improving their ability to draw better things to themselves.

One man imagined light around himself when he was with a difficult client who was making unreasonable demands and complaining loudly. Rather than trying to appease his client, he imagined light all around himself, made his own energy as beautiful as possible, took a deep breath, and sent the client light through his heart. Within several minutes the energy between them changed dramatically, and the client became more reasonable and calm.

Another man's wife left him unexpectedly, taking their children and moving out. He felt devastated, as he loved his wife and children. Although he didn't believe it would work, he called light to himself every day, and sent his wife love. Rather than pleading with her or getting angry, he called light to himself when he was with her. Before moving out, she had acted cold and distant. As he worked with light, she became softer and more responsive, and within two months she returned.

You can change your future by imagining what you want to happen, and adding light to the picture. You can think of a future date—a day, month, or year—and send light to that time. Light will make everything you experience at that date better.

Light is a powerful source of healing.
If there is any place of discomfort in your body,
send it light.

You can call upon light to heal your body. Take a moment to get quiet and tune in to your body. Is there any place of discomfort? Focus on that place, and get a clear image of the pain. How

CREATING WITH LIGHT | 23

large or deep is it? Now, think of light, and call it to you. Put light around the area of discomfort. As you do, ask that part of your body if there is anything else you can do that would assist it in letting go of this pain or discomfort.

A woman with severe back pain went to several doctors who were not able to find any physical cause. She began sending light to her back, and she not only felt less pain after a while, but each time the discomfort came back it was less severe. As she increased the light in her life, she also realized that she was feeling burdened, trying to make everyone happy, and feeling as if everything would fall apart if she let go for even a minute. She was "wearing the burdens of the world on her shoulders" and feeling that she was carrying everyone on her back. She changed her attitude and decided to let others learn their own lessons, rather than trying to save them or live their lives for them. With that shift, her back pains completely went away. To her surprise, things did not fall apart and the people around her began taking more responsibility for making their own lives work.

You may want to heal others, but not know how to do so in the most effective way. The more radiant you become, the more you will be able to assist others in their growth simply by your increased light. You can also assist them by sending light to them. As you do this, you increase your own radiance even more.

To heal others with light start by drawing in as much light as you can imagine and putting it all around you. Then imagine yourself as clear as a crystal, so that you are a pure transmitter of light. Send the other person an image of light. Imagine light going out from your hands, your heart, or the top of your head as if you are sending a stream of light from you to him or her. That is all that is necessary; your Higher Self will handle all the details. You need only to have the intent to send healing energy as you transmit light, and you will.

A friend of Sanaya's called from a hospital to say that another friend had been in an accident and was critically injured. She wanted our assistance for the friend. I instructed Sanaya to call light to herself, surround and charge herself with light, and when she felt full of light to send it in one strong burst to the woman in the hospital. Several other people were with Sanaya, and they were asked to do the same thing. The friend in the hospital would be able to use this light for whatever purpose served her higher good: either to get well or to die peacefully and go to the light. Everyone got quiet and sent a burst of light. The friend called back ten minutes later to report that almost immediately the woman's vital signs had changed for the better, and she was no longer hanging between life and death.

If anyone you know is in pain—emotional, mental, or physical—you can assist by sending light every time you think of him or her. Thoughts of others often come into your mind because at a deep level they are asking for your love and light.

The light you send to others will come back to you multiplied.

Increasing the amount of light you can hold and radiate is a great gift to yourself and the world. As you become more radiant and charged with light, people will be drawn to you. Those who are ready will shift to a higher consciousness simply by being in your presence.

All the light you send others will come back to you multiplied. Send light through your eyes by imagining light going out through your eyes when you look at another person. Imagine light going out through your hands as you touch another person. You can do this whenever you see someone who could use assistance—when you are standing in line at the grocery store or post office, when you are with friends, or whenever you remember to do so. Every moment you spend sending out light increases your radiance. As you make your energy beautiful, charge yourself with light and then radiate it, you are being your Higher Self.

Creating With Light

MEDITATION

The purpose of this meditation is to learn how to call light to yourself, charge yourself with light, and radiate light.

Steps: Get into your Higher Self state for this meditation.

1. To call light to you and charge yourself with light:

   a. Imagine making your energy as beautiful as possible. Imagining you are doing so is all that is necessary to make it beautiful. As you are making your energy beautiful, make any physical shifts in your posture that make you more comfortable, allow you to breathe deeply, and let the energy flow along your spine.

   b. Take a deep breath and invite light to come to you. Light is a living consciousness that responds instantly to your call. Let it come into your spine; imagine your spine as a rod filled with light extending above your head and below your feet. From your spine, radiate light outward to your body. Imagine adding lines of light throughout your body so that you can hold more light at a physical level. Send light into your cells, to your DNA, and then into the atoms in your body. Completely fill your body with light.

   c. Make this light the most beautiful color you can imagine. What color is it? Is it a golden light, or do you imagine a white or bluish-white light? Make this light's intensity and radiance just right for you.

d. Imagine this light as a sphere or cocoon all around you, in front and back, above your head and below your feet. Extend this light beyond your body into the room. Make your sphere of light so large it fills the whole room or beyond. Then, make it so small it fits very close to your body. Decide how large you want your sphere of light that feels just right. Does your sphere have a defined boundary, or does it just gradually fade out? If it has a defined boundary, where in the room does this light stop?

2. Radiating light:

After you have called light to you and charged yourself with light, you can send light to many different things. You can send light to your ideas, the future, your higher purpose, your body, thoughts, and feelings. You change the energy of whatever you send light to into a higher, finer vibration. Radiate light when you are in a situation you want to change, or send light to other people to assist them.

a. Think of a person you want to send light to. Start by sending light to this person through your whole body. Notice how it feels. Next imagine light coming out of your eyes, hands, or heart and going directly to this person. Use the way of sending light to others that feels the most comfortable and right to you.

b. Think of something you want to send light to. Call light to you and charge yourself with light. Imagine yourself being as clear as a crystal, so that you are a pure transmitter of light. Then, send light to whatever you have chosen. Next, send energy through your heart and then through your whole body to this thing.

Use the way of sending light that feels the most comfortable and right to you.

c. Think of other things you want to send light to, such as world peace, the earth, animals, or whatever you like. Notice that as you send light your own light becomes brighter and more beautiful.

d. You have now learned how to call light to you, charge yourself with light, and radiate light.

3

Connecting With the Universal Mind

Everything around you exists as part of the Universal Mind, also called God/All-That-Is. The Universal Mind is unmanifest essence—the substance out of which all physical form is created. You are part of this Infinite Intelligence. This Higher Intelligence exists in perfection and perfectly creates your thoughts, beliefs, and inner pictures as the world you experience around you. You can learn to tap into this Higher Mind and draw to you unlimited health, abundance, new ideas, knowledge, and anything else you want.

The Universal Mind is perfection.
It perfectly creates what you think about.

How can you best use your connection to this vast, all-powerful force? Think about what you want rather than what you don't want, for the Universal Mind creates whatever you think about. Focus steadily on your visions, hopes, dreams, and goals, and intend to have them. Allow your mind to come under the direction of your Higher Self and have clear, positive, and creative thoughts.

Imagine that your reality is in truth only a dream you are having. You have embellished your dream with certain props— your home, job, and material possessions—all reflecting what you think you can have. You draw to yourself other people who play out complementary roles, acting as mirrors to teach you more about yourself. You are here to learn about your thoughts and emotions, and you learn by seeing them reflected all around you.

Since your reality is YOUR dream, you can dream it any way you want. You can change the script anytime you want, bring in new actors, and make your dream turn out a better way. You can have everything you want that serves your higher good. Your reality is not as rigid as you might believe; you can change your circumstances more easily than you might think. You can have a world of joy, smiling faces, peace, abundance, and more; there are no limits to what you can have.

You can create miracles by doing "energy work."

How do you connect with the Universal Mind and use this connection to create what you want? You are always linked with the Universal Mind, for It creates whatever you think about. You can learn to consciously link with the Universal Mind by doing what I will call "energy work" before you take physical action to create what you want. The Universal Mind contains the unmanifest essence of all forms before they appear in your physical reality. As you work with energy you are consciously working with the Universal Mind.

Energy work involves using thought, imagination, and visualization before you take physical action. Energy work uses the power of light, magnetism, and your link with the higher dimensions to create results.

You can do energy work by using your imagination to turn what you want into patterns, colors, symbols, or a feeling-sense. You do energy work by then imagining the pattern to be more beautiful, open, and harmonious. As you mentally picture and play with the image of what you want to create, you are working with it as energy.

When you do energy work and then add light, there is no limit to what you can create. Doing energy work before you take physical action will bring the events, circumstances, and things you want into your life more rapidly and in better ways than when you don't. Working directly with the essence of what you want will bring things to you in their highest form. Creating with energy can produce such immediate and powerful results that many would call it "creating miracles."

Before you do energy work, first concentrate on the results you want to create. Then, imagine your mental aura as a gridwork of light, extending straight upward. The higher it goes, the finer the gridwork becomes. Some people picture this gridwork as a screen whose mesh grows finer the higher it reaches. Others see it as a fabric of woven light, imagining the weave to be closer and finer in the higher dimensions.

Send your awareness upward through this gridwork and imagine that you are linking with the higher aspects of the Universal Mind. Imagine you are meeting with what you want to create in its energy state, and mentally work with whatever image comes into your mind to make it more beautiful. When it feels good as energy, you can "draw" it into your reality by imagining you are turning this energy into subatomic particles of light that you harmonize with and bring into your being. You can learn to do this within seconds, and doing this can create amazing and rapid results.

For example, one man was waiting in a long line where everyone else was irritated and impatient at the wait. He started to improve the situation by concentrating on the results he wanted—that the line move more quickly and the people feel at peace. He then imagined a gridwork of light around his head extending straight upward, becoming finer and more beautiful the higher it went. Using his imagination, he imagined what the results he wanted would look like as energy. He saw pink circles of harmony spreading outward. He added light to this image. It took only seconds to do this energy work, and he was amazed at the results. Immediately after he finished, three people in front of him decided to leave, two clerks came and opened up new lines, and everyone became calmer. He was served and gone in minutes.

When it was time to get my first book, *Living With Joy*, published, I had Sanaya do energy work instead of sending the manuscript to publishers. She started by picturing the result she wanted—a published book.

During one session of working with the book as energy, she imagined it looking like a magnetic ball of light that called to itself all the people who wanted to add more light to their lives and whom this book would assist in doing so. Another time she imagined the manuscript charged with the energy of everyone who would be assisted by reading it, letting a publisher be drawn by the possibility of making a contribution to the lives of these people.

Though Sanaya enjoyed working with the unpublished book as energy, she also felt concerned, thinking that she should take some concrete physical action. Since no particular action seemed to be indicated, she kept working with energy and didn't send the manuscript out to publishers. She didn't know that a friend had given the manuscript to a publisher. One day, while meditating, the publisher got a very strong inner message that he was to publish the book, even though he hadn't thought of doing so before. He immediately called Sanaya to tell her of his decision, and the book was published.

When you work with energy it may feel as if you are "making it up." You can create real results by imagining you are working with the energy of what you want to create. For example, one woman was trying to rent a car because hers had broken down and she needed a car to drive to work and pick her children up from school.

A friend drove her to the airport where she talked to representatives from each of the many rental car agencies there. They all told her the same thing—that they couldn't rent a car to her because she didn't have a credit card. She was ready to give up, but because she desperately needed a car, she tried to think of something else to do. She remembered that she could consciously link with the Universal Mind and work with what she wanted as energy.

She went outside and took a moment to concentrate on the results she wanted—to drive away in a car she had rented. Next, she imagined her mental aura as a gridwork of light. She sent her awareness upward along it into the higher dimensions, where she sensed the energy of what she wanted. Everything felt very closed and rigid, so she mentally pictured the energy opening up. She put light around everything until she felt an almost physical "click." It felt like she was making it up, yet she felt drawn to go back to one agency that had turned her down. She discovered that a new representative had come on duty. He found a way for her to rent the car, telling her he didn't know why he was making an exception other than that for some strange reason he felt compelled to assist her.

One man wanted to attract more clients to his business. He had tried advertising and many other things, but most of the promotions cost him a lot of money and brought in few clients. He decided to work with what he wanted to create—more clients—as energy. He sat quietly, sending his awareness upward along the gridwork to connect with the Universal Mind and the energy of what he wanted to create.

He imagined a rainbow going from his heart to each person he wanted to reach. He made the picture even more vivid and powerful by imagining beautiful music playing as he connected with each person. He sent an image of light to each person from his heart to theirs, and told them mentally how he would welcome and serve them as his clients.

Within a week many new clients contacted him, even though he had done no additional advertising. Several new ideas came into his mind about how he could attract more business, and when he took action on them he was able to dramatically increase the number of clients he served.

One company found out that a valued employee was quitting and immediately went to work to replace her. They put ads in a newspaper and shortly thereafter hired someone. This person found another job the day before she was scheduled to start working for them, and the next person they hired never showed up or called on the day she was supposed to start. They decided they needed to do energy work before they placed any more ads.

Though some did not believe it would work, they all sat together and focused on the person for whom the job would be ideal. They created a clear, fine gridwork of light around all of them, and imagined going upward into the higher dimensions to create a welcoming, inviting space for this person to come to. Each person contributed his or her picture of the energy needed, and they took turns playing with each person's images. The next day a person who had seen the ad in an old newspaper called about the job. She turned out to be perfect for the job and was soon happily employed with their company.

Another group of people felt that their office was too dark and gloomy and their boss was too restrictive. They felt they got too little positive feedback and that their ideas were ignored. They had complained about these things, but nothing had changed. They decided they needed to work with the situation as energy.

Together they imagined a fine gridwork of light around themselves, extending into the higher dimensions of the Universal Mind where the conditions they wanted existed as energy. They first pictured their office and their current conditions as a small, dark cage that they then turned into an auditorium filled with light. They kept playing with this symbol until it felt expansive, flowing, and open.

Within a month, things changed dramatically in ways they couldn't have predicted. Their negative and restrictive boss quit, and her replacement was a very supportive and positive person. The head of the company suddenly decided to move the office to a larger, more open, and light-filled place. After the move, their boss changed internal policies so that each person had more say in how decisions were made.

> *The more expansive your thoughts, the more expansive the reality you create.*

Your creativity and imagination are two important keys in making a better reality for yourself. You need to be creative to work with things as energy, and you need to use your imagination to picture the results you want. When you use your creativity and imagination, you can expand your ideas of what is possible for you to have and thus create a better life for yourself.

You can learn to be creative. All of you have experienced moments of creativity—sudden insights, new visions of the way something could be done, and bursts of inspiration. The only differences between people who think they are creative and people who think they aren't are their beliefs about their creativity. Start telling yourself that you are a creative person.

You have the ability to generate new ideas that will take you to higher levels in your life and work. Stop for a moment and think of something you would like to improve. Then, be creative and picture something even better than you have yet imagined happening in this area. Don't accept your current circumstances as the best you'll ever have. Don't believe people when they tell you something is impossible to create. When you know how to create with energy and light, anything is possible.

Believe in your success.
Picture yourself having what you want.

Learn to use your imagination. Your ability to picture something that does not yet exist in your reality is one of your highest abilities. Your imagination allows you to think of having more than you have now. Your imagination transcends this dimension and connects with the Universal Mind where anything is possible. Your imagination can connect with what you want as energy, play with it, add light to it, and then bring it into your reality quickly and easily.

Take time to daydream, fantasize, relax, and think about what you want to create. Practice thinking in new, unlimited ways. Unlimited thinking puts you in touch with the larger picture of your life and links you with the expanded vision of your Higher Self. Enlarge your vision of what is possible. Think positively, and imagine yourself having more than you have now.

If you want a relationship to be more loving, picture that relationship as you want it to be rather than focusing on the way it is. If you want money, abundance, your soul-mate, or good health, imagine you already have whatever you want and thank your Higher Self in advance for bringing it to you. Work with the energy of what you want and believe it is possible to have.

Use affirmations, positive statements in the present tense that affirm you already have what you want. For instance, you can say, "I am now enlightened; I now have abundance; I am loving, kind, and open," and thus become these things. Although these things may not be true while you are saying them, as you continue to say these things they will become true.

Trust that once you affirm having something, everything that happens is preparing you to have it. As you picture your success and affirm that you already have it, the Universal Mind works with you, creating perfectly for you the things you think about and believe in.

The Universal Mind can create FOR you only what It can create THROUGH you.

You are a co-creative force with the Universal Mind. It creates for you the best that is possible within the boundaries of your current ability to receive what you are asking for. If you think in expanded, creative, and open ways, the Universal Mind will reflect this by giving you the more expansive things you think about. You can have the best life you can imagine—a life filled with joy, abundance, loving friends, and good health. Think of an area in your life you would like to improve; take a moment right now to picture it just as you want it to be. Affirm that what you want WILL happen, and trust that it will manifest for you in the perfect time and in the perfect way. Create it as energy, and use the meditation that follows to bring it into your life.

Connecting With the Universal Mind

MEDITATION

The purpose of this meditation is to connect with the Universal Mind and bring something you want from the world of unmanifest energy into physical form.

For this exercise, think of a specific thing you want, something that is a definite object or thing, not a relationship or a quality such as inner peace.

Steps: Get into your Higher Self state for this meditation.

1. Imagine a gridwork of light around your head, extending straight upward into the higher dimensions. The higher it goes, the finer and more beautiful the gridwork becomes. Send your awareness up along this gridwork and imagine you are leaving your earth reality and going into the world of essence that is the Universal Mind.

2. See yourself meeting with the unmanifest energy of what you want to create. Use your imagination to picture it. Does it have a pattern or color? Can you sense or feel it? Can you make it into a symbol?

3. Make the image more flowing, open, and harmonious. Enhance it even more, perhaps adding color, fragrance, and beautiful sounds. Make its colors and its patterns more beautiful. Make it a size that feels good. Imagine that the unmanifest energy of what you are creating is alive and let it interact with you. Now add light to it. If you are working with a symbol, interact with this symbol.

4. You are now ready to bring this into your physical world. Let the energy of what you want change into subatomic particles of light. Create the particles with as high a vibration as you can imagine. As you change its energy into particles of light, see it crossing from the world of essence into your world of form. Let these particles of light begin to coalesce. Imagine them having a shape and mass as they come together.

5. Open your heart to receive these light particles that represent the energy of what you want. Greet them with love and embrace them as you draw them toward you.

6. Bring these subatomic light particles into your DNA located in the center of every cell. Feel the light particles penetrating all your DNA, which are encoded with your life's program. Imagine your DNA are now cooperating to bring this thing into your life in its highest, most enlightened form. The light particles of this thing are harmonizing with your life through your DNA so that it comes to you easily and fits into every part of your life.

7. Radiate light particles of what you want from your DNA into all your cells, and then to your emotions and mind.

8. Pretend you already have this thing in your life. How do you feel now that you have it? Imagine you are creating a time and space for it. How much space does it take? How close in time are you putting it?

9. Thank what you want in advance for coming. Affirm that you are ready to have it in your life. Be ready to receive it and recognize it when it comes. As you return to the room, feel your new connection to this thing you are bringing into your life.

4

Linking With the Higher Will

The Higher Will is an aspect of God/All-That-Is. It is a moving current of energy that carries everything in the direction of higher evolution. It is a gentle stream of love and spiritual energies that leads everything in all kingdoms—mineral, plant, animal, and human—to growth, aliveness, and a higher order of being.

There is a divine plan to the universe. This plan does not exist in the form of guidelines about the specific forms and actions that are to be taken to carry it out. It exists as spiritual energies. The Higher Will is stepping up the frequencies of these energies with great precision to move your physical world and all consciousness in it toward their highest evolution. You have complete free will to react in any way you want to these energies. If you want to use them to grow spiritually, they will greatly assist you.

If you want to connect with this current of evolution, simply be willing to have your life take on a higher order. Be open to allowing and accepting good things into your life. Believe you deserve to have the best life you can imagine. As you align with the Higher Will, your life will become more harmonious and satisfying.

The Higher Will is the will to do good and to serve and assist others. You can strengthen your alignment with the Higher Will by asking, "How does creating this contribute to the higher good of myself and others?" The more you broaden your thinking to encompass serving others, the more you attune with the Higher Will. As you serve others, you gain rewards and a richness of spirit that go beyond anything you could imagine. That is what the Higher Will is all about—creating the highest good for everyone, for that will be for your own greatest good as well.

> There is a higher purpose to your life,
> a special contribution
> you came to make.

Part of your reason for coming to earth is to evolve yourself as well as to serve humanity in some way. We will call the process of evolving yourself your "life purpose," and the service you came to offer humanity your "life's work." They are intertwined, because as you serve others you will naturally evolve yourself. As you evolve and radiate more light, you automatically serve others. Everything you do to evolve yourself and carry out your life's work is an act of aligning with the Higher Will and your Higher Self.

You have a special role to play, something that you are uniquely fitted for. Your life's work will take on various forms at different times. The form may change from month to month and year to year, so keep in touch with your purpose and vision as it expands and grows. You can discover your life's work through examining the skills you love to use, the things you love to do, and the areas you are naturally drawn to. Whatever you love to do will also serve others in some way, for it is the nature of the universe that when you use your highest skills you automatically contribute to others.

Your dreams about your ideal life are showing you your potential and higher path. Don't discard your dreams and fantasies as merely wishful thinking. Honor them as messages from the deepest part of your being about your life's work and what you came here to do.

You knew that during your lifetime there would be new frequencies and energies established upon the earth plane that would carry greater love, order, and harmony than in the past. You knew that a new wave of energy and light would be present during your lifetime. You came to aid in bringing those new energies into every level of society, and you are drawn to the particular area of work where you can best establish these new energies.

You can know the Higher Will by listening within.

Aligning with the Higher Will will guide you to take the actions that will produce the results you want. After you have done your energy work and before you take physical action, stop for a moment and imagine you are joining the higher current. You might imagine a higher stream of energy that leads to your goal, and picture yourself joining it. Imagine that you are being joined by the Higher Will and that It is assisting you in creating whatever is for your highest good in the best and fastest way possible.

Your Higher Self is linked with the Higher Will and is always sending you guidance about how you can flow more with the universe and ride the higher current. As you take time to listen within, you will become more aware of the guidance your Higher Self is sending you in the form of thoughts and feelings. You can use this guidance to create many positive results in your life.

Take action only when your feeling is inviting, open, and positive. Then the actions you take will be aligned with the Higher Will. You will need less effort to get positive results. For instance, after you have done your energy work to create results, you may have an urge to call someone. Before you call this person, stop for a moment, get quiet, and imagine yourself calling. If calling feels warm, good, and inviting, then call. If you feel resistance, if your energy drops, or you have any other negative feeling when you think of doing something, wait.

A woman who was in sales called people only after she took a moment to get quiet and wait for the feeling that it was a good time to call. Through a process of trial and error, she became good at recognizing which feelings she had when it was a good time to call and which she had when it wasn't. When it was appropriate to call, she usually had a welcoming, inviting sense as she thought of the person she wanted to call. When she didn't have this feeling but called anyway, people turned out to be busy, in bad moods, not available, or closed to her ideas. When she waited until the energy felt good to call, she usually had a good, productive conversation.

To align with the Higher Will, develop an awareness of your energy, of the people around you, and of how you feel from moment to moment. Only take action when there is a definite, positive feeling to do so. Your feelings and awareness will tell you if you are in the higher flow. If you are aware that your energy is closing down or that you aren't feeling high, you will know that you have lost the connection to the higher flow. Whenever your energy feels vibrant and alive you are following the Higher Will.

You can align with the Higher Will by listening to your inner messages. Your Higher Self is always guiding you to be aligned with the Higher Will. As you learn to tell the difference between the inner guidance you receive from your Higher Self and the messages you receive from your intellect, you will be able to create what you want more rapidly and joyfully.

Messages from your Higher Self are loving and gentle.

One way you can tell the difference between the messages from your Higher Self and the messages from your intellect is to note if there is any fearful thought behind the message. Messages from your intellect are often based on thoughts of scarcity, guilt, or a need to protect yourself from some imagined threat. If you are asking for guidance and want answers, do not pay attention to answers you receive that are based on fear, for they are not from your Higher Self. The messages from your Higher Self will allow you to feel peaceful and balanced.

Higher Self guidance is often subtle and quiet and is frequently the message that follows the first one you hear. Your intellect may quickly jump in with answers, so when you are reflecting on what action to take, the first or loudest answer you receive may not come from your Higher Self. To receive messages from your Higher Self, get silent, and wait until you sense an answer that is reassuring and loving.

For instance, after you have worked with the energy of what you want to create, you may wonder what physical action to take to get the results you seek. Your intellect may jump in and tell you why you need to take a certain action to protect yourself, or tell you it isn't possible to have what you want. You know that any fear-based message is not from your Higher Self, so you keep listening. As you continue to listen, you will hear your Higher Self's message, which may be telling you that everything is all right, not to worry, and not to take any immediate action. The quiet voice of your Higher Self is always encouraging and positive.

Your Higher Self guides you to the higher flow through your heart. If you have a choice to make, choose what you are drawn to and would love to do. Take the action your heart is leading you to. Do not force yourself to do things. If you catch yourself saying, "I *should* or *have to* do this," doing it is not for your higher good or aligned with the Higher Will.

Your Higher Self is always sending you suggestions and ideas to keep you flowing in the higher current and linked with the Higher Will. These suggestions are very gentle. You are rarely asked to make radical changes without many suggestions of simpler changes first. Sometimes insights about changes you need to make may be quite surprising. However, your Higher Self will show you how to create these changes using your current skills, resources, and capabilities.

Take time to relax and become aware of your inner messages. Do you give yourself a good balance between times when you are quiet and able to think and times when you are busy and active? If you are active all day long, continually pouring out energy, do you also allow yourself "breathing spaces"? If you don't feel that these two states are in balance, what one thing could you do today or tomorrow to bring them into balance? Taking time to be quiet and listen to your thoughts and feelings is just as important as all your busyness.

You can greatly increase the joy and ease of your life by taking time to think about things in a calm, peaceful state before you take action. Sometimes one simple idea can save you months of hard work or prevent a major problem. Never feel guilty for taking time to think. As you take the time you need to think things through, your life will become more peaceful and will work in better ways.

You are a co-creator with the Higher Will.

You are here to work with the Higher Will; you are the one who carries out your work and makes a difference in the world. Aligning with the Higher Will doesn't mean becoming less of an individual. Your individuality, strength, perceptions, and uniqueness assist you in effectively carrying out the Higher Will and purpose of your life.

Don't wait for fate to decide what will happen to you. Alignment with the Higher Will requires you to set goals, decide on the results you want, and take action. You have a highly developed will for a reason; the more you have learned to use your will wisely, the more able you are to create your higher path and effectively carry out the actions that are indicated.

How do you know if you are exerting too much or too little force? How do you know if you are exerting your own will against the Higher Will? If you are trying to create something and you must struggle, push, and work hard to force things to happen with little result, you are not following the Higher Will.

A *few* obstacles may come up to provide you with the opportunity to become stronger and more definite about your goals. However, if you continue to find too many "closed doors," if you feel exhausted or drained by your efforts, or feel you are doing something only because you have no other choice—STOP. Look for something else you have been wanting to do. When you are flowing with the Higher Will, there is a balance between feeling carried by the current and feeling that you are using your own will to create results.

When do you let go, surrender, and let things happen, and when do you use your will and become an active force? It is always appropriate to do energy work and then take whatever actions appeal to you. If you want a particular result, do everything that your inner messages are indicating. Then, surrender and let the best happen.

If, after you have done your energy work, there appears to be no clear action or strong feeling to do anything, it is usually better to wait. Surrender and trust that what happens—even if it doesn't meet your expectations—is perfect in some way for you and your growth.

When you are linked with the Higher Will and are in the higher flow, you will feel good at a physical level. Your body will feel relaxed and comfortable and have plenty of energy. If you discover that you aren't feeling this way, stop for a moment, breathe deeply, and ask for a message about how you could be more in the flow. Listen to the quiet message from your Higher Self, for there is usually an easier way to do things.

Things happen easily when you flow with the Higher Will.

You are meant to live a joyful life. You are here to create your dreams; you can create a heaven on earth for yourself. You deserve to have the best life you can imagine. Do what you love and follow your heart in every area of your life, for as you do, you are aligning with the Higher Will.

Linking With the Higher Will

MEDITATION

The purpose of this meditation is to energize your reaching your highest evolution and potential in this lifetime by aligning with the Higher Will.

Steps: Get into your Higher Self state for this meditation.

1. Close your eyes and sit quietly. Ask your Higher Self to show you a symbol that represents your highest evolution for this lifetime. Take whatever picture comes to your mind, for it will be the perfect symbol to energize at this time. What does this symbol look like? Imagine you are standing in front of this symbol. Picture energy coming from your Higher Self and going directly into your symbol, energizing it. Surround your symbol with light.

2. Imagine you are placing this symbol on top of a mountain. Connect it to you with a path that stretches in front of you all the way to the top. What does this path look like? Choose the path to the top that looks the most inviting, from a slow, winding one to a steep, direct path.

3. See yourself joyfully going up this path all the way to the top of the mountain. You are balanced and calm on your journey. You have a vision and you are always guided by it.

4. Now imagine yourself at the top of the mountain. Congratulate yourself on your single-minded dedication to your purpose. Imagine how you will feel as you manifest

your highest potential, become enlightened, and radiate light to others.

5. Stand in front of your symbol and imagine linking with it. Imagine this symbol radiating light and energy throughout your body, until every cell is aligned with your spiritual growth and higher purpose. Bring the symbol into your heart, merging completely with it. Then release this symbol to the Higher Will.

6. Feel your unity with the Higher Will. You might envision a cord of light coming out of your solar plexus, the area above your navel, linking your will with the Higher Will.

7. There is a broadcast coming from the Higher Will of humanity's path of highest evolution. Imagine you are tuning into this broadcast and aligning all your energies with the Higher Will, the path of humanity's highest evolution, and your part in it. Your higher purpose and life's work will now unfold in a greater way and everything you do will be in alignment with the higher current.

8. Continue to enjoy the view from the top, as well as the good feelings you are experiencing. You may stay as long as you like. You have just energized your higher purpose and joined the higher current of the Higher Will.

5

Seeing the Bigger Picture: Receiving Revelations

Seeing the bigger picture involves putting everything into its larger framework, where its true meaning can be understood. Imagine you are working on a jigsaw puzzle. You put pieces together in one corner and you can see a small house. You may work on a completely different area next, and a tree may appear. They don't seem to be connected until later, when you work on another part and a country scene unfolds. The tree and the house are complete within themselves, but they are also parts of the bigger picture.

You may have already discovered that seemingly unimportant things you learned, jobs you took, and experiences you had all fit together in a way you couldn't have anticipated at the time. It was only later, when you saw a bigger picture, that you realized the importance of certain things. Your Higher Self has a larger plan for your life, and every experience you have will fit together and give you value in some way, even if you don't yet know how.

As you link with the Higher Will you will learn more about the bigger picture of your life and the part you will play in the grand scheme of things. Those who perceive this bigger picture are often called "visionaries" because they have broader visions than most people. You too will become a visionary as you learn to see the bigger picture of your and others' lives. As you see the larger picture of what is happening to humanity, you will know more clearly how you can serve and what contribution you can make.

Imagine you are standing surrounded by a heavy fog. It is so heavy all you can see is a few trees near you. The fog begins to lift, and you can see that you are on a hill. As the fog continues to lift, you can see more hills in the distance, and you soon have a complete picture of all the surrounding areas. This is what it is like as you see the bigger picture; you have an increasingly clear view of the world as seen through the eyes of your Higher Self. With this larger vision, much of your spiritual growth will come from within and be self-directed.

Spiritual growth comes as a series of revelations.

The earth plane has been called "dense" by some. The density of matter creates a veil of unknowing, and once born here most people, even highly evolved souls, lose their memory of who they are. You must often operate "blind," with only a dim awareness of your purposes and goals. This is one of the reasons your dimension offers such a challenge—and so much opportunity for growth.

The knowledge and wisdom of your Higher Self comes through a series of revelations. Revelations are those moments when the veils lift and you have an insight, breakthrough, or new understanding. As the veils lift you will see beyond this reality and receive many insights into things you might not have even thought about before.

As your Higher Self connection grows stronger, you will become more aware of Its greater wisdom and perspective. You may have unusual thoughts and questions. You may wonder about or receive insights into life on other planets; your own past lives; and the nature of reality, time, and space. You may feel drawn to explore and learn about things you were never interested in before.

Revelations are a stripping away of the temporary not-knowing and a gaining of the knowledge of your Higher Self. Revelations provide you with information about the greater reality you are a part of, the higher plan for humanity, and your higher purpose. Through a series of insights, you will gradually learn more about your path, your mission, and your next steps.

Revelations will show you why things are happening from a higher, wiser perspective. You will gain a greater understanding of people and events. You will gradually discover the meaning of life, the purpose of the universe, and the "why" behind the "what." Each revelation will lift the veils between your dimension and the higher ones and give you more pieces of the bigger picture.

As the veils are lifted, you will gain an expanded vision of your life and the universe. This knowledge will be of higher truths that have always existed but are unknown to you until you are ready to open to the larger, more unlimited perspective of your Higher Self.

Seeing the bigger picture will show you the perfection of the universe. You will understand cause and effect. You will begin to know at a deep level that everything you are doing is perfect. You may realize your discomfort in some area is moving you toward a goal. You may recognize that feeling off-balance and off-course is a part of learning how to feel balanced and on-course. You might have an insight that your illness is simply your body's way of balancing and bringing itself to a higher vibration or helping you move to a new level of self-love. Seeing the bigger picture will give you the inner peace and confidence that comes from knowing the universe works in perfect ways to bring you your higher good.

You can increase your ability to see the bigger picture and receive revelations by asking yourself questions such as, "Why am I here? What am I here to do?" Use your imagination to ask questions that bring you revelations about the nature of the universe. Think of questions that invite answers that give you a bigger picture. Ask such questions as, "Where do I come from? What happens to me after I die? Is this the only planet with life? Do I travel and live in other dimensions? Have I lived other lifetimes?"

As you grow spiritually, you will understand your life purpose.

Think of the activities in your life right now. Ask questions such as, "What is the true meaning of this activity? How does it fit into the larger picture of my life? How is what I am doing adding more light to the world?" As you ask these questions, you will learn more about how what you are doing now relates to your life purpose. You may have insights about how everything you have done in the past fits together with what you are doing now.

You can receive much information about your specific life purpose and how you may carry it out simply by asking for this information. You are here for many reasons. There are many lessons to learn, higher qualities to develop, and a special contribution you came to make to humanity. The meditation that follows this chapter is a journey to the Library where the Akashic Records containing your and others' soul records are kept. This Library exists in the higher dimensions of the Universal Mind, and you can reach it by using your imagination. The Akashic Records contain the records of all your lifetimes.

Revelations often come when you are in a relaxed state. Thomas Edison got many of his best ideas when he took his small "naps" during the day, relaxing his body and turning off his normal awareness. For years Albert Einstein asked questions about the nature of time and space that led to his discovery of the theory of relativity. His breakthrough came in a dream in which he saw himself riding a beam of light to the end of the universe; the way the light traveled gave him the breakthrough he was looking for.

Revelations can come in moments of reflection, through meditation, while taking a walk, or even in the shower. Revelations are creative breakthroughs that give you new insights about the nature of reality, new visions of what is possible, and a greater understanding of what is happening in your life.

Revelations can be simple or complex. They usually carry a special feeling with them; some of you get goosebumps, tingling, or other physical sensations. Sometimes you have no physical sensation, but you feel a mental "click," as if a piece has just fallen into place. You can receive revelations in many ways—directly into your mind as insights, from channeling, from reading a book, or by hearing something.

One woman wanted to know more about why she was born and why she had chosen her particular parents. One day while she was sitting and listening to music, she got the message: "You came to develop an open heart. You chose to be in all the circumstances that closed your heart in the past, in other lives. You chose parents who didn't know how to love you, criticized you often, lacked time to spend with you, and acted in ways you had judged impossible to love in other lifetimes. Yet, because they were your parents and you were their child, you found it in your heart to love them, and thus grew spiritually by learning to love behaviors you had previously judged unlovable."

Revelations challenge you to believe in the ideas you receive rather than thinking you made them up. When you reach a certain level of spiritual development, much information will come through your mind and inner senses.

Nurture your ability to receive insights and revelations by believing in them. When an idea that is new or different comes into your mind, you might think of it as a tiny seedling that is just breaking through the soil. It will grow stronger if you say to yourself, "This idea might be possible to manifest, it might be true, the universe may work this way," and so on. You can be the gardener of new ideas, nurturing them and encouraging them to develop.

Learn to trust the insights you receive.

When a revelation first comes, it may not be fully formed. You may get a glimpse of something and feel that your understanding of it is just out of reach. Revelations usually appear first as unformed, fragmented thoughts. Let new ideas flow through you without trying to make sense of them or have them perfect in your first attempt. Play with your insights. You will understand more about them as you receive gradual and steady additional insights that build into a complete picture.

Some ideas may come to you with a flash of great excitement, showing you new ways to live your life. At first you may not see ways to carry them out, but as you play with them a pathway will appear by which you can get from where you are now to where you want to be. Although it is important to take action on your insights, you will not want to start until your ideas are complete enough so that you can successfully carry them out. As you think about these ideas, they become more complete. You begin to draw to yourself the circumstances, coincidences, and people to bring them into your life.

You may feel as if you have been on a quest, searching for answers and meaning. You may wish that you could have everything revealed to you at once. You need to receive revelations at a pace that is comfortable to you, for if information is revealed too soon or too fast it may cause confusion or require you to change your existing belief systems in too drastic a way to make sense of it. Trust that you are receiving as much understanding of the greater reality as you can handle right now.

If you receive too much information all at once, you may reject it. You may be able to think of an idea you now consider normal that you once rejected because it seemed too unusual. Each time you receive a revelation it needs to fit into your existing belief systems and current understandings. Some revelations challenge you to open to new views of reality and see your life in different ways. To receive more insights, start by becoming as flexible and open to new ideas as possible.

It *is important to use your insights*
to make your life work in better ways.

When insights and revelations first come to you, they may bring a sense of release, excitement, and joy. This high, stimulating feeling may be followed by a time when the excitement fades. You now have the task of carrying out your insights and fitting them into your life.

For instance, you may receive a series of revelations about your life's work and a new direction you need to take with your career. You may decide you need to reexamine your current job and possibly take new actions. You may have many exciting ideas about how your new path will create good for you and others, and feel much enthusiasm about acting on your insights.

After your initial excitement about your new career path, you will need to carry through with whatever actions are indicated. It is not enough just to receive revelations; you grow by carrying them out. The creative ideas you receive will take you to new levels of personal growth and expression as you implement them. Putting your insights into action may require you to do new things, learn new skills, take risks, and venture into the unknown. Manifesting your new path will challenge you to expand your potential, be creative, and think in different ways, for this is the nature of revelations.

Learn to take action on insights and ideas when they show you how you can live a better life. The process of manifesting your insights brings spiritual growth; mastering the process is as important as accomplishing your goals. People who don't take action don't gain the benefits their insights and revelations are meant to bring them. Implementing your insights gives you the skills you need to create a better life, have more abundance, and feel greater aliveness.

Don't look to other people for validation, for you will be receiving ideas that are new and just beyond the mass thought. At some point, everyone you know may applaud you and tell you what a great idea you have, but do not wait for this support to believe in and act upon your ideas. Develop the courage to believe in yourself and your insights. Do things as you see best, not as others tell you to.

Have you had insights recently about something you need to take action on? Ask yourself what step, even a simple one, you could take to put this insight to work for you. When combined with action, insights and revelations create powerful results. Ideas alone are not enough to create your success in this world; you need to trust your ideas, apply them, and persist in carrying them out.

Life becomes easier when the bigger picture of your life and the meaning of the universe become known to you. You have a guiding vision. When you see the bigger picture, you can do much in a short period of time, for you will know what actions to take that create the greatest results. You will know where your energy and time can do the most good. Seeing the larger picture will make the daily, practical things you do more joyful, for they will have greater meaning as you know how they contribute to the bigger picture of your life.

Seeing the Bigger Picture

MEDITATION

The purpose of this meditation is to journey to the Akashic Records to learn more about yourself, including why you chose this lifetime, what your higher purpose is, what lessons you came to learn, and more about your service to humanity.

The Akashic Records are kept in the Library, a place that exists in the higher dimensions beyond the physical world. The Akashic Records contain information about your and others' lifetimes, information about your growth, your life's goals, and more.

Steps: Get into your Higher Self state for this meditation.

1. Call light to you and imagine a cocoon of light all around you. Make the light beautiful and the cocoon of light just the right size that feels good. You might imagine this cocoon is like a bubble that you can ride in. Imagine yourself floating higher and higher, being carried into the higher dimensions in your bubble, until you are at the Library.

2. You are standing in front of the Library. What does it look like? When you are ready, enter the Library and look around. You can see row upon row of books, representing information about your and others' lifetimes.

3. You are met by a very high being, who greets you warmly. Mentally tell this being you want to view the records of your lifetimes. Upon making this request you immediately find yourself in front of your Higher Self's records,

for in the higher dimensions as soon as you think of something, you experience it.

4. These books contain information about the goals, purposes, and contributions of all your lifetimes. Pull out the book that contains your records of this lifetime. What does it look like? When you are ready, open this book and look at the first page. The first page has a dedication to the essence of your life's work and the contribution you came to make in this lifetime. What is written here?

5. Turn to the next page. Here you will find more about your life's work and the contribution you came to make. Let yourself imagine what is written here.

6. As you turn to the next page, you find the qualities you are working on in this lifetime—such as love, courage, trust, and compassion. What are some of the qualities you are currently working on developing more fully?

7. If there is anything else you would like to read about, do so. What are some of the important events in your life that have been recorded? What are you working on now that is most important when viewed from the perspective of your Higher Self?

8. When you are ready to leave, imagine you are outside the Library once again. Put light all around yourself, and let your bubble of light carry you back to where you are right now. If you want additional information about your life, you can return to the Library anytime you want.

6

Opening Awareness of the Inner Planes

There are other realities that exist besides the reality you can see, touch, and hear with your physical senses. These are the higher dimensions that your Higher Self lives in. These realities are very real; your Higher Self, other people's Higher Selves, and many high beings live there.

The dimensions your Higher Self normally exists in are made of vibrations that exist at a higher frequency than your physical world. Everything in your world has a vibration—the atoms in your body, your home, and the food you eat. What makes matter solid and real for you is the relationship between the rate of its vibration and yours. The higher dimensions are separated from yours in part by their vibrations; they have faster, smoother, and higher vibrations. As you grow spiritually you increase your vibration, and the dimensions of your Higher Self become more knowable and real to you. Because these realities are knowable through the inner world of your thoughts, imagination, and inner senses, I will call them the "inner planes" of reality.

There is a spiritual community
of many high beings who work
together on the inner planes.

As you become attuned to your Higher Self, you also become aware of the dimensions your Higher Self exists in. You
can consciously join with the higher community of beings your
Higher Self is already a part of.

Part of the higher purpose of the community of higher beings
is to work with the Universal Mind and Higher Will to assist all
life in evolving. They work continually to assist people in awakening, working with the Higher Will to broadcast spiritual
energies. They help make the journey easier for all who are
seeking growth, serving others, or requesting assistance. You
can become more aware of the work that is going on in the
higher dimensions to carry out the plan of evolution. With this
awareness, it will be even easier to know and carry out your
own higher purpose.

Some of these beings act as guides and work intensely with a
particular person besides contributing in other ways. Other
beings contribute in various ways to assist all who are open to
and asking for assistance. Every call for help is always heard.
Light and assistance is immediately sent from both your Higher
Self and these high beings. Every resource is made available
and nothing is spared when you ask for assistance. If you could
only know how much love there is for you in the higher dimensions, you would never feel alone or worry again.

There is no feeling of separateness in the higher realms. All
beings contribute wherever they can create the most good, just
as you work together with each other to create important things
in your reality. Sometimes your Higher Self will work with you
on something; other times your Higher Self will work together
with high spiritual guides to empower you and assist you with
your life's work and spiritual growth.

In the higher dimensions there is never criticism, only mutual respect and kind words. There is gentleness, humility, and a focus on the work that is to be done. All beings hold a high vision for each other and send each other unconditional love. There is no thought of the self that doesn't also include the well-being of others.

If anyone is working on a project, it is everyone's concern. There is no feeling that one must do it all alone. All work receives the energy support of all. There is never a thought of scarcity or competition; all is viewed to be a part of the divine and perfect order of the universe. It is an inclusive group and all can join who want to be of assistance. There is still a sense of individuality in the dimensions your Higher Self lives in, yet the individual is connected to all other beings in a much greater way than in your reality.

Your connection to these higher dimensions comes through your higher centers of telepathy. Most of you receive telepathically through your emotional centers. You experience this when you are around people and "pick up" what they are feeling. Part of spiritual growth is learning to become transparent to the emotional messages of others, and opening your higher centers of telepathy so you can receive guidance from your Higher Self.

Your higher telepathic centers are mental and intuitive; you receive clear mental guidance or an intuitive sense of what to do through these centers. You automatically open your higher centers of telepathy as you align with your Higher Self and hear and follow Its guidance.

You can use your higher centers of telepathy to send messages to the Higher Selves of others or become aware of the soul-level consciousness present in other life-forms—such as plants, animals, and minerals. Through higher telepathy you can become aware of the many high beings serving mankind, your own personal guide if you choose, and the dimensions of your Higher Self.

You can connect with any of these high beings by imagining you are connecting with them. If you are working on a project, ask for extra guidance and assistance with it. Imagine light is being sent to you, your work, or your loved ones. You are not alone; there is much assistance, support, and empowerment available for you and your world-work when you connect with this higher community.

You can work in the inner planes by becoming inner-directed rather than outer-directed.

As you live as your Higher Self, guidance and information will come from within rather than from without. Guidance from your Higher Self is received in your higher telepathic centers and transmitted to you through your imagination and mind. Since your connection to the higher dimensions comes from within, pay attention to your thoughts, inner senses, and imagination.

Meditation is a powerful tool for becoming aware of these higher dimensions and your Higher Self guidance. Meditation allows you to quiet your normal thoughts and listen to your Higher Self. It allows you to pay more attention to your inner reality of pictures, images, and feelings. As you meditate you increase your vibration and frequency, and the dimensions of your Higher Self become more knowable to you. Meditation increases your sensitivity to ideas, concepts, and images from the higher realms and your Higher Self.

Meditation can involve states of relaxation, observation, and concentration. Meditation can take many forms—from silencing your mind to concentrating on a project. Meditation is an inner reflective attitude, a time of concentrated thought. You are meditating when you are focused and thinking about how you can assist others or carry out your life purpose. Meditation can consist of sending light and love to people or sitting quietly and silencing your mind. Things that allow you to relax, concentrate, or silence your mind—long walks in the woods, listening to music, and sitting quietly and thinking about things—will connect you with your Higher Self and the higher dimensions.

You can increase your ability to connect with the higher dimensions by learning how to relax, focus, and concentrate. You do not need a formal meditation practice to achieve this; you can learn by practicing on your daily activities. In the same way, you can practice silencing your normal stream of mind-chatter during your daily activities and achieve a state of meditation even while you are active. As you become one with your Higher Self you will have a steady spiritual focus that will allow you to be constantly in touch with the higher dimensions as your primary reality. You will not need to sit for hours and practice formal meditation; for you will be in a state of meditation—active receiving, inner listening, and focused awareness—no matter what you are doing.

You can sense energy in crystals and other life-forms such as plants and animals.

As your Higher Self, you are connected with the soul consciousness of all life-forms through the inner planes. You can learn to consciously connect with the souls of minerals, plants, and animals by using your imagination and abilities of higher telepathy. As you become more aware of your inner world you will be able to know your oneness with and understand the consciousness of other life-forms. You will still maintain your individuality and sense of self. Feeling unity and oneness means having the ability to experience life from the perspective of whatever or whomever you are focusing on. You will gain compassion, wisdom, and a deeper understanding of yourself as you learn how to see life through the "eyes" of other life-forms.

You can use your imagination to connect with other life-forms. Next time you are near a tree, sit quietly by it and pretend you are the tree. As you pretend to be the tree, tune in to the other plants as you imagine they would appear to the tree. How does the tree experience night and day, heat and cold? How does the tree experience you? As you do this, you may sense subtle feelings, impressions, and images that go beyond words.

This is the beginning of becoming one with all life and experiencing this aspect of your Higher Self's consciousness. You can pick up images from the tree and sense to some degree its reality, because you and the tree have a unity at a deeper level. With your mind and imagination you can become one with and gain a greater understanding of the consciousness of a rock, tree, plant, or any animal you tune in to. Don't worry if you feel you are making it up. Trust the impressions you receive.

You can become aware of the consciousness of a crystal. At this time, many of you are drawn to the mineral kingdom and particularly to crystals. This is because their molecular crystalline pattern increases your ability to tune in to other dimensions through the inner planes of reality. The inner planes consist of a gridwork of light that is very similar to crystalline structures. Having crystals nearby can increase your ability to transmit energy telepathically and to work in the inner planes and higher dimensions.

You can send and receive telepathic messages through the inner planes.

You can make a contribution to world peace or assist others telepathically by sending light to them or to all of humanity through the inner planes. As you do, you increase the amount of light in the world as much as through any physical effort.

You might picture the inner planes as a vast network of a very orderly, fine gridwork of light. The higher the dimension, the finer the gridwork of light. Messages can travel along this gridwork from your Higher Self to the Higher Selves of others.

You can send telepathic messages to people you know. Messages sent from your Higher Self to another person's Higher Self will bring results. Think of someone you would like to communicate with. Get quiet, and imagine a fine gridwork of light around you, extending straight upward. Next, imagine a line of light going out from your heart to this person's. Mentally tell this person you love and accept him or her exactly as he or she is. Express any other messages of love you want to send.

One man did this with his wife when they were having conflicts over one of their children. He felt she was being too lenient and she felt he was too harsh. They had reached an impasse; neither was willing to budge. It even got to the point where they weren't talking to each other. He sent his wife a telepathic message through the inner planes from his Higher Self, telling her he loved her and wanted peace between them. Soon after he sent his message, his wife came to say she was open to a new solution, and they arrived at a mutually agreeable compromise.

In these times of planetary change, people are changing rapidly, and new forms, ideas, and information are flooding the planet. If you try to find stability in the outer world you may feel confused and uncertain. As you go within and connect with the higher dimensions and your Higher Self, you will find love, stability, and peace. A constant broadcast of peace, success, and spiritual focus; and other expressions of light are always available. All you need to do is get quiet and imagine you are tuning in to this broadcast to receive it.

Not only are there high beings in the inner planes, but also there are many different and beautiful places within these planes. For instance, there are places where the pure notes of love, compassion, courage, and other qualities exist. Each place holds one constant note, such as joy, broadcasting it throughout many dimensions. These places are composed of energy, sound, light, and vibrations. You can mentally travel to them and absorb the qualities they emit. They act as a reference point for the pure vibration of that feeling-tone throughout many universes. Anytime you want more of these qualities you may travel to these places and absorb more of whatever quality you desire.

Sometimes you may feel an overwhelming urge to get quiet, followed by a sense of energy or force pouring through you. These are the times when your Higher Self is doing great world work, assisting in sending light and energy through the inner planes. Respond by getting quiet and letting this high vibration of energy pour through you. As it does, your radiance will grow even brighter.

As you open your awareness to the inner planes, you will be increasingly sensitive to telepathic impressions from the higher realms and your Higher Self. You will gain an increasing ability to assist people telepathically and to receive guidance and assistance for yourself. You will have a greater role in carrying out the Higher Will and will become more aware of the greater evolutionary plan for humanity. You will be valued as a member of the higher communities that are assisting all humanity and life to reach their highest potential, and given much support and love for your spiritual growth and life's work.

Opening Awareness of the Inner Planes

MEDITATION

The purpose of this meditation is to open your higher centers of telepathy and to meet the higher community of beings who are working together on the inner planes to assist all who are awakening or asking for guidance.

Steps: You might want to have a crystal nearby that you can hold in your hand.

1. Call light to you and imagine light all around you. Imagine you are in a bubble of light and it is carrying you to a temple where there are many high beings. These high beings are working together to lift the vibrations of humanity and align all people with their Higher Selves. They are broadcasting peace, love, and spiritual awakening.

2. Feel the peace, love, and joy that are all around you as you arrive at the temple. Notice how beautiful the temple and surrounding grounds are. Listen to the sounds of nature and the beautiful undertone of chanting.

3. Your Higher Self walks over to you. Feel the unconditional love, peace, and tranquility radiating from your Higher Self to you. As your Higher Self stands before you, It touches your crown center, at the top of your head, to help you awaken spiritually. Your Higher Self then gently touches your third eye, located on your forehead between your eyes. This opens your inner vision even more and

aligns both centers with the vibrations of your Higher Self.

4. Your Higher Self now leads you to a beautiful courtyard where many high beings are sitting in a circle. They are sending out a broadcast of peace, love, and joy that is available to all who are listening. You and your Higher Self are invited to join this circle and sit in the center. As you sit, you tune in to their broadcast. Feel the love and joy pouring through you. Anytime you want to feel better all you need do is imagine yourself sitting in this circle, receiving this broadcast.

5. Feel the warm welcome sent you and the joy everyone has at your joining this higher community. Everyone is sending you love and support for your work and spiritual growth. Bask for a moment in the love and light that is being sent you.

6. Three very high and powerful beings come forward and stand around you and your Higher Self, forming a triangle. You are being held in their light, empowered and loved. Feel how loved you are. Many more beings come and stand around you in ever-increasing triangles. In this light, feel yourself merging once again with your Higher Self. You are now your Higher Self.

7. These beings now gather into a larger circle, and you are invited to join them to send light to the plant kingdom. As you send light, mentally ask the plant kingdom if there is anything you can do right now to assist it, and ask how the plant kingdom might assist you in your growth. When you finish, imagine doing the same thing with the animal kingdom.

8. You are now going to join with all these beings to send light and love to the mineral kingdom and the earth itself. You might want to hold your crystal and imagine light flowing through it to the earth. Feel your love and connection to the earth. Ask how you might assist the earth right now, and how you might strengthen your connection to it for your growth.

9. When you are ready to leave, thank these beings for their light. Let your bubble of light carry you back to the room you are in. Feel the increased connection you now have with the higher community of beings, the plant, animal, and mineral kingdoms, and the earth itself.

7

Moving Into Higher
Consciousness

As you become your Higher Self, you will experience many
higher states of consciousness. These states come naturally
with your increased observation, attention, and awareness. They
come from your greater attunement with the higher dimensions and your growing ability to exist in more dimensions
than just your earth reality. They come as you grow more fluid,
believe that anything is possible, and open your mind to explore the unknown.

As you become your Higher Self you may experience increased psychic and telepathic abilities, clairvoyant sight, and
past-life memories. It is not necessary to develop these abilities
to grow spiritually, but these abilities may be a part of your
growth. You can develop them consciously, or you may experience them occurring naturally as you grow.

You can consciously develop skills of higher consciousness
by increasing your awareness. Everything you do has more
levels to it than you usually pay attention to. There is much
more going on around you than you are normally aware of. As

you become more observant and aware, you will notice the subtle energies that exist all around you; they are always present and you can work with them to change your reality.

How many levels can you be aware of at one time? Can you notice your breathing, your posture, your thoughts, emotions, muscle movements, sounds in the room, the feeling of your clothing on your body, and smells around you all at once? How far into the room does your energy extend beyond your body? Feel the richness of your ability to sense subtle energies.

As you become more aware, you will bring the consciousness of your Higher Self into areas that used to be unconscious. You may have vivid dreams or dreams that give you messages and guidance about your life. As your awareness increases, you may be aware of other lives you have lived, such as parallel and past lives. Past-life memories may begin surfacing. For instance, when you meet people for the first time you may take an immediate liking to them, feeling as if you have known them before. You may go somewhere new and feel as if you've been there before.

As you become your Higher Self, you may have a greater awareness of your psychic abilities. You may find yourself knowing things without knowing how you know them. You might find yourself anticipating what people are going to say before they speak, or even completing sentences for them. You may have a sense that something is going to happen, and it does. You might think of someone and run into her or have her call shortly afterward. You may get flashes of information about someone you don't even know and find out later your information was accurate. Although this information is always available to you, it becomes more noticeable as you grow and gain the awareness of your Higher Self. This awareness lets you become more aware of your thoughts and everything going on around you.

Developing the increased awareness and sensitivity of your Higher Self—such as clairvoyant sight and telepathic and psychic abilities—gives you more personal power and perspective.

With increased clairvoyant abilities, you gain another dimension of consciousness that will let you operate even more powerfully in your normal reality. You will understand how to consciously create results that once seemed like miracles. You will gain an increasing ability to heal yourself, stay centered and balanced, know who you are, and increase the positive energy around you.

How you use these abilities will determine whether or not they serve your higher good. They will contribute to your spiritual growth if you use them to serve and empower others and as tools to create your life purpose. They will not serve your growth if you use them to control others, to falsely build up your ego, or as goals in themselves. These abilities are tools to nurture your growth, not the goals of growing.

Your clairvoyant abilities will increase as you become your Higher Self.

Your clairvoyant abilities—your abilities to sense, see, and hear information beyond what is available to your physical senses—will increase and allow you to become more sensitive to these subtle energies. Many of you are already having experiences with clairvoyant sight but don't know what to call it. For instance, you may have looked at someone and intuitively known that something was wrong with him or her. You may touch someone and feel drawn to move your hands in a certain way without even thinking about it. The way you move your hands might create a release or shift for that person. You may find yourself gesturing with your hands as if you are moving energy while you talk. You may be able to sense a cold or illness coming on before you have any physical symptoms.

You may sense other people's physical, emotional, and mental energy bodies. You may also be able to sense where people's energy patterns lack harmony. Some people see disruptions in other people's energy with their inner eyes as places of greater density or darkness. These may indicate places where there is illness or where the person has taken on energy patterns from another person that aren't in harmony with theirs.

As you grow, you will discover more about your own energy systems. You will learn how to work with energy to heal yourself and even transmute food in your body. By working at an energy level you can create dramatic changes in yourself. Start developing your clairvoyant sight—the ability to work with your energy bodies—by trusting your imagination and being playful, inventive, and creative. For instance, if you feel a cold coming on, pretend you can see your aura—the energy surrounding your body—as it extends out and away from your body. Notice if it doesn't look or feel right somewhere. Don't worry if you can't really see it; pretend you are seeing it with your inner eyes.

Some people imagine that their energy fields appear collapsed or too close to their bodies if there is physical pain or illness. Some sense colors. You might begin by imagining you are expanding your energy field so that it looks beautiful and balanced. Then make the color more beautiful, or add colors. Send light to this area as well. Be as playful as you can until you feel a shift. The key to creating a lasting change is your ability to observe even the slightest temporary changes. Congratulate yourself even if the change in the physical feeling lasts only a second or two. Any change is an indication that you are on the right track and that what you are doing is affecting your energy.

One man had a sore throat. He was a singer and had a performance coming up. He did not want to lose his voice. He began using his imagination and pretending he could see bands of light around his throat. Some seemed too compressed, so he imagined pulling them out. Immediately he felt more pain and constriction, so he stopped using that image.

He hadn't really believed working on his energy would produce any results, so the immediate changes were encouraging to him, even if they were in the wrong direction. He then imagined adding more bands, making them finer, and adding light. His throat began to feel much better, although only for seconds at a time. He woke up several times during the night and kept playing with the sore throat, using his imagination. His feeling of well-being lasted longer and longer. When he woke up the next day his sore throat was gone.

As you develop these powers of higher consciousness you will gain a larger and larger perspective of the universe. Your beliefs and thoughts about what is possible will change. Your ability to affect matter and produce physical results will increase. As you are able to influence people and things with greater skill, you will discover your sense of responsibility increasing simultaneously. All these powers—telepathy, clairvoyance, and enhanced psychic abilities—will give you more clarity and knowledge to assist others to reach their higher wisdom also. It is important to develop them at just the right rate for you and to use them with the highest integrity.

Moving Into Higher Consciousness

MEDITATION

The purpose of this meditation is to assist you in developing your abilities to sense the subtle energies of the higher dimensions and to further stimulate your psychic center known as the "third eye" and your spiritual center known as your "crown center."

Steps:

1. Sit in a comfortable position. Become aware of the sounds in the room, the feelings of your clothing against your skin, and the rhythm and fullness of your breath. Breathe deeply a few times, then send your awareness through your body and make yourself as comfortable as you can. As you relax even more, observe your heartbeat and pulse.

2. Imagine you are merging with the radiance and light of your Higher Self. As your Higher Self, focus on your emotional body. You might imagine that your emotional body feels like a layer of energy just on the surface of and outside your physical body. As your Higher Self, "pull" your emotional body farther from your physical body until it stands around you sparkling, fluid, and clear.

3. Now picture your spiritual center on the top of your head as a lotus flower. Each time you grow and reach upward, a petal unfolds, until you have a thousand-petaled lotus. Imagine what you will feel like when all the petals are unfolded. Picture the lotus as it looks right now—how many of the petals are open? Imagine more petals opening

gently and easily. As they open, picture yourself being surrounded by the shimmer of your awakened spiritual body.

4. Next imagine the gridwork of light around you that is your mental body. Extend it straight upward, and make it finer and more beautiful.

5. As your Higher Self, put a violet light around your pineal gland, located behind your eyes near the center of your skull. The pineal gland regulates the awakening of the spiritual eyes that can see subtle energies in this dimension and others, including seeing your and others' auras.

6. Look around the room with your eyes soft-focused. Be observant of any differences from what you normally see or any greater awareness of the energy around the things you are looking at. If you notice a soft glow around things, play with looking into the glow to see more about it—its size, density, any patterns it contains, and so on.

7. As you come back to the room, congratulate yourself for working on your energy centers and being willing to see more of the unseen, subtle energies around you.

Doing this meditation may increase the development of your clairvoyant sight. Clairvoyant sight develops at its own pace and in a way that is comfortable to you. Acknowledge each time you have a greater inner awareness of those energies that used to be invisible or unrecognized, for you are becoming aware of the higher dimensions and seeing things through the eyes of your Higher Self.

SECTION II

Opening Inward

8

Raising Your Vibration

Raising your vibration comes from opening your heart. When you feel loving, you experience more aliveness, expansion, and renewal. Love is flowing with the universe rather than resisting it. Love is a willingness to be vulnerable; it is accepting yourself and others just as you and they are. Unconditional love dissolves all separateness. As you learn to love yourself and others more, you increase your vibration. Your energy takes on the smoother, finer vibrations of the higher dimensions and you become your Higher Self.

Love is the doorway to enlightenment.

You can open your heart more by loving yourself. Love all the parts of yourself, even those thoughts and feelings you may have labeled as negative. If you feel anger or doubt, love those feelings as much as you love your feelings of joy and peace.

Love your humanity as well as your divinity. Love your insecurities and your negative feelings. If you feel unforgiving or unloving, love those feelings too. Love all of what you call your "imperfections." You don't change them by denying or hating them. You change them by loving them. As you love your negative feelings they can evolve into their positive expressions.

Love all your thoughts, even those that are limited or fearful. Think of them as small children needing your love and reassurance. If you catch a negative thought, don't make yourself wrong for having it. Love all your negative thoughts and they will have far less power over you. If you are imagining things you want to stop thinking about, love yourself for thinking them and it will be easier to stop. Put a positive thought alongside your negative thought; one positive thought can cancel out hundreds of negative ones.

One woman was afraid of elevators and heights. She hated herself for feeling afraid, and had tried to talk herself out of her fears. Nothing seemed to work until she decided to try a new tactic—to love her feelings. The next time she got on an elevator she felt panic but kept sending love to her fearful feelings. As she rode upward they grew less strong, until at the top floor she felt a rush of elation and expansiveness.

You can love your negative feelings, and thus raise their vibrations out of limitation into light, or you can hate and resist them. Hating them gives them even more power over you. Love your humanness; it is what you are here to experience and learn from. Love your weaknesses as well as your strengths, for those are the areas that most need your love to evolve. As you love your negative feelings, your world expands and your choices increase.

Love creates healing.

Illness is created by a contraction of energy. Contraction occurs when you aren't loving to yourself. For instance, if you catch a cold it may be a sign that you aren't loving yourself enough. If you feel a cold coming on, ask yourself what nurturing thing you would do for yourself if you had a cold. You might take a rest or let go of some of the pressure you are under. Promise yourself you will do those things even if you don't have a cold—and often your cold will go away. Of course, be sure to do what you promised!

In longer illnesses, you may have noticed that there was a shift in your thoughts and feelings at the point when you started getting well. You create some illnesses to provide you with the opportunity to release old energies and move to a new level of self-love. When you love and honor yourself more, you raise your vibration, and the course of any illness changes.

Most healing by a true healer takes place because the healer has a higher vibrational pattern of love and more life-force energy than the person being healed, at least in the area that is causing the illness. The healer's energy field extends outward and creates a space for a person to love himself or herself more. As he or she does, the area that is contracted and causing the illness expands, which creates the opportunity for healing to take place.

You strengthen people as you surround them with your loving thoughts.

As you love and accept yourself, extend the same feelings to others. People are doing the best they know how given their backgrounds, circumstances, and beliefs. Rather than judging or criticizing other people, ask yourself what you can do to make their lives better. A group of women friends were critical when one of them began drinking more and neglecting her children. They realized they needed to be more loving, so they asked themselves what they could do to assist her. Rather than trying to change their friend in any way, they began to mentally broadcast to her a message that they loved her just as she was. Then they began sending her light. The results were dramatic.

Two weeks later, she suddenly decided to quit drinking and turned her life around.

Send people loving thoughts. As you do, you strengthen them and support them in attracting good things. Great masters spend much of their time in states of deep love, sending energy and love telepathically to those who are asking for assistance.

You can send love backward and forward in time and it will have a beneficial effect, for love transcends time. One woman sent love and forgiveness back to an old boyfriend. He had rejected her and hurt her feelings many years before, and she occasionally still thought of his rejection and felt hurt. She imagined herself talking to his Higher Self, sending him love and forgiveness. Shortly afterward she noticed a shift in her relationship with her husband; she was able to be more open and vulnerable, as if she was no longer protecting herself from rejection. If there is anyone in your past who wronged you, or whom you wronged, send love and forgiveness back to him or her. As you do, you will raise your vibration.

When you go to a new level of love and commitment with people, they may start acting in unlovable ways they hadn't expressed before. Love is a powerful energy. The parts of a person that have not felt loved in the past begin to feel safe enough to expose themselves. Your love creates a safe place for healing to take place. If someone has become harder to love after you have become more loving, realize that it is only happening *because* you have become more loving, not in spite of it.

All *negativity is a cry for more love.*

Everybody can use more love. Do not take offense if people are rude or unkind or seem like they are trying to hurt your feelings. You cannot know what is happening with them. Send them love no matter how they act. It will come back to you many times over as increased love in your life. As you love others, even those things about them that are unlovable, you rapidly increase your vibration.

One woman went to a drugstore and the pharmacist was very rude to her. She was tempted to snap back at him, but instead kept sending him love. When she left, she wanted to send him bad thoughts, but didn't. She also forgave herself for having bad thoughts about him, which made it easier to send him loving thoughts. Several weeks later she went back to that drugstore, and the pharmacist acted very differently. Not only was he friendly, but also he confided to her that several weeks before he had found out his wife had cancer and might not have long to live. Upon discovering these hidden facts, she felt glad she had sent him love and not bad thoughts.

Many of the people you are dealing with are younger than you at a soul level and aren't yet able to act kind and loving as often as they would like. Learn to stop reacting to others' unkindness, rudeness, or lack of consideration for you. Reacting with hurt or pain simply takes you out of your calm, clear center. Send a thought of forgiveness and be loving and kind to everyone, no matter how they behave. Love yourself even if your response isn't as high as you would like.

Love regenerates the cells in your body and lets you rise out of the density of the earth plane. If you see ugliness, love that too. If you see others behaving in mean, unfriendly ways, love them. Rather than criticizing others or focusing on their faults, realize that you have the opportunity to raise your vibration by loving them. As you open to love, you will experience a more beautiful world all around you.

You attract things and people of a similar vibration.

Because everything in your universe has a vibration, the rate of your vibration determines the people, events, circumstances, and objects you draw to yourself. Loving others, then, is really a gift to yourself—for as you love them you raise your vibration and thus attract better things.

You may feel righteous or superior to your loved ones, feeling that your spiritual growth makes you the better person. All people's Higher Selves are equal, though people have different levels of ability in expressing their Higher Selves in their earth lives. You may say, "My partner doesn't meditate or eat the healthy food I eat. He/She isn't as loving, balanced, stable, logical, or clearheaded as I. Therefore, he/she isn't as high as I am." Realize that you are with the partner you are with because you have a similar vibration.

You attract friends and loved ones whose soul development and lessons are similar to yours. There will be areas where your loved ones are more developed than you and areas where you are more advanced than they. You may increase your vibration to a level where you are no longer at the same point of development, and if this happens you will probably separate. In the meantime, as long as you are with people, view them as equals, even if they don't do the things you think spiritually evolved people "ought" to do. When you feel superior or righteous, you contract your energy, close your heart, and lower your vibration.

Raising your vibration changes your relationship to everything. Since your personal objects are attracted to your vibration, when you change your vibration you may go through periods of selling things, losing things, or buying new things. You may look in your closet and decide none of your clothes feels right any more and you want new ones. You may move to a new home or city.

Your increased vibration also changes your self-image. As you change your identity, you may lose those things that symbolize old parts of your personality. For instance, if you lose your wallet, you may be letting go of the identity symbolized by your driver's license or other cards you carry.

You may also go through periods when things around you break down. Electrical appliances are particularly susceptible to changes in your vibration, as the rate of your vibration affects your electromagnetic energy field. You may have several electrical items break down at the same time. You can end this pattern of things breaking down by establishing new connections to all your objects. Just imagine you are connecting with them as you do when you first buy things—play with them, admire them, or handle them with love. You can walk into a room and imagine you are sending lines of light to all your objects, reconnecting with them at your new, higher level.

Your higher vibration lifts the energy around you.

When you bring your energy to as high a note as you can, you set the vibratory tone for the surrounding environment. Others cannot help but pick it up. Think of a time when you were around a person who was very loving, peaceful, and focused. You probably felt more loving, peaceful, and focused yourself.

Your Higher Self exists in a state of love. Every time you are loving, kind, forgiving, and compassionate to yourself and others, you are being your Higher Self. Learn to love everything in your life—every feeling, thought, and action you take. Think of yourself as a beautiful, loving person, doing the best you know how to grow and evolve.

Raising Your Vibration

MEDITATION

The purpose of this meditation is to open your heart center and use your awakened heart to open and balance your energies at many levels from the physical to the spiritual.

Steps: Get into your Higher Self state for this meditation.

1. Put your hand over your heart, and say to yourself with feeling: "I love you. I accept you as you are. I commit to you. You are important. Your life counts." Say this until you can feel its truth.

2. Ask your heart to guide you to follow its loving way. Ask it to speak to you more clearly. Tell it you will listen. You can trust your heart, for it will always lead you to your higher good. Put your hand down gently.

3. Imagine your heart as a star, and let it radiate love and light to every cell in your body. Feel the light from your heart balancing, harmonizing, and regenerating your body, enhancing the flow of life-force energy throughout.

4. Spend a moment feeling any emotions that are present right now. Send love to each one you can identify. Take a moment to listen to your thoughts as they come into your mind. Send love to each thought as it comes up.

5. As you come back to the room, take a deep breath and feel the glow of love throughout your body.

9

Calming Your Emotions

At an energy level, there is still much turbulence on your earth plane. The wave patterns in your universe have not yet lost what might be called the "violence of creation." In the higher realms, the wave patterns are smoother and calmer. Part of your purpose on earth is to bring these calmer, smoother energies to the earth plane, assisting in the evolution of matter.

You might feel this turbulence most strongly in your emotions. Learning to calm your emotions is an important step in becoming your Higher Self. Strong and heavy emotions take you out of your peaceful center and make it harder to hear the quiet voice of your Higher Self. Can you imagine what your life would be like if you always felt calm, centered, and balanced? You might still have strong feelings to do things, but they would be harmonious, balanced feelings rather than turbulent ones.

Emotions focus you in time and space. Your emotions are the fuel that propels your thoughts into manifestation; your feelings of wanting something make it easier to bring it into your life. Though you need to have a feeling about something before you can create it, you can create things from positive, harmonious emotions rather than from negative or disharmonious ones.

Part of your journey into your Higher Self is to learn to hear and act upon Its guidance. When your emotions are calm, you will hear this guidance mentally, take action, and find your life flowing smoothly. When you don't follow the whispers and guidance of your Higher Self, you may find things growing harder. You may create circumstances that trigger strong and turbulent emotions. Strong, intense emotions signal you that you are not following the path and guidance of your Higher Self. The further away from your Higher Self you are, the harder things become and the more intense and turbulent your emotions may be.

For instance, one man kept having thoughts that he needed to change his job. He didn't take action, however, and soon felt increasing resistance to coming to work. He started to feel bored and restless, but still didn't take any action. The feelings intensified, and he began to dislike his job so much he developed minor colds and illnesses that allowed him to stay home. His performance suffered, and one day he was fired. He immediately took action to get a new job. To his amazement, he found a wonderful job right away. He realized things would have been much easier had he left his old job when he first had the guidance to do so, and he wouldn't have experienced so many turbulent emotions.

To grow with joy, it is important to follow your inner messages and make small, easy changes. Then things will not get so out of balance and you will not create situations that trigger strong, intense feelings.

If you are feeling a negative emotion about something, ask your Higher Self what guidance you need to hear to make things work more smoothly in this area. *Every* negative emotion signals you that there is a message from your Higher Self you need to pay attention to. When you hear the message, you can take the actions your Higher Self is guiding you to take and change the situation that is causing you turmoil.

If you feel a negative emotion, stop and ask your Higher Self, "What is the message? What do I need to look at in my life or do differently?" Learn to pay attention to the slightest feelings of irritability, resentment, or negativity. Is there any area you consistently have negative feelings about? Stop for a moment and ask for a message on this area.

Your highly evolved teachers have not gotten rid of their emotions, for emotions are part of the human experience. However, their emotions are peaceful and harmonious no matter what is going on around them. They listen to their Higher Self guidance and create harmony and clarity all about them. As you achieve greater levels of mastery, you may still recognize a flash of anger or irritation, but you will learn to process these feelings in an instant, ask what guidance you need to pay attention to, and let them go.

You *have one prominent emotion called your "birth emotion" and several satellite emotions.*

There are many currents of energy going through you in the form of emotions. One is your birth emotion. It is a deep feeling that you have carried throughout your life. Although every cell and atom in your body is different from when you were born, unless you have undergone a major spiritual transformation, you still carry this core feeling with you.

Some of you choose optimism, happiness, or complacency as your main feeling-tone. Others choose an underlying feeling of pessimism, resentment, or disappointment. Some have an easygoing nature; others feel a quiet melancholy, loneliness, or unhappiness. Some people choose love as their main feeling-tone; others choose to be serious or fun-loving. Some choose smug superiority; others choose to feel unworthy and inferior.

Think for a moment about your most prominent feeling. Are

you normally happy, easy-going, or optimistic? Are you tense, worried, or unhappy a lot? If you don't recognize your most noticeable feeling-tone right now, simply be aware that you have one and ask to know more about it. You may sense it as an inner note rather than a distinct feeling. Besides a prominent feeling-tone, you have five to seven satellite emotions that make up your prime emotional identity in this lifetime. What emotions do you feel most often?

Your Higher Self chose these particular emotions to lead you into certain experiences you would not have without them. Your emotions are the lenses through which you look out at the world. When you are happy you see the world differently than when you are angry or sad. Experiencing each emotion is like putting on a new pair of glasses; every feeling shows you a different way of looking at the world. You chose these emotions because they gave you the perspective that would provide the most growth for you.

You chose the range of intensity of your emotions. Some of you have chosen a very broad range, from immense pain to great joy. Some of you have chosen narrower ranges, preferring to work with subtle levels, such as moderate joy to moderate unhappiness. Because you live in a polarity, for each positive emotion you have you will also have its opposite. Emotional calm comes from finding the balance point, bringing all your emotions into harmony with your Higher Self.

You have a lot of daily emotions, and most of them are fleeting. If you think back to the feelings you have had today, you might recognize at least two or three different ones. Emotions are like a moving force-field; you can experience them and then let them flow right through you. It is important not to identify with them or hang on to them longer than necessary to gain their gifts. Any that take you out of your center are showing you that in some way you are not flowing and in touch with your Higher Self.

Some of you feel more alive when you have strong, turbulent emotions. You may worry that calming your emotions will make you feel less alive. For instance, if things are too peaceful with your mate, you may think that your relationship has lost some of its passion and aliveness. You may be confusing intensity with love. Some people think that unless there is a lot of emotional drama in a relationship, the other person doesn't care for them. They love high, intense feelings and create dramas in order to feel them. What images and thoughts come up for you as you think of being calm all the time?

Some of you learn to value harmonious emotions by first experiencing turbulent ones. You may be angry or cry for hours, feeling hurt, betrayed, or rejected. You will come to a point where strong, negative emotions are intolerable and you want peace above all else. With that strong desire you will begin to make the changes that will bring calm into your life. Are you ready to let go of the drama? If so, say to yourself, "I choose peace."

Love people for who they are, not for who you want them to be.

If your turbulent emotions are coming from upsets in your relationships, look closely—are you accepting other people for who they are? Or are you withholding your love until they become who you want them to be? You always win by supporting other people in being who they are rather than who you want them to be. Usually, when you release your attachment to wanting people to be a certain way, they become more cooperative and loving.

Your most intimate relationships involve your greatest expectations and present your greatest challenges to being calm and centered. If your loved ones are upsetting you, ask yourself, "Why am I reacting this way? What pattern within me are they triggering? Does this situation remind me of something hurtful from the past? What am I learning from this turmoil?"

If you feel disappointed with the way people are behaving or treating you, rather than assuming that you have done nothing to cause their behavior ask, "What am I doing? Am I making them defensive? Am I demanding that they act in certain ways to please me? Am I making what they do wrong in any way? Am I accepting and loving them for who they are?" Knowing how your words and behaviors affect others makes it easier to create the reality you want with them.

Once you feel hurt, many of you become protective and closed, wanting to be certain you are not going to be hurt again. From now on, whenever people are doing something that upsets or hurts you, see it as an opportunity to learn to love them rather than protect yourself. Send love to your feelings of hurt. Realize that others' behaviors that hurt you are coming from their fear of being hurt themselves, not from their intent to harm you.

One man was continually upset over his relationship with his wife because he felt she neglected him. He had many specific things he thought she should do to prove she loved him, such as being home every night, watching television with him, and staying home with the children rather than working. She truly loved him and tried her best to please him, but she also wanted a career and wanted to go out occasionally. She became increasingly silent and withdrawn as he grew more angry. One day, in a moment of inspiration, he decided that he was contributing to the turbulence and began to think about how he could change.

He asked himself why her behavior upset him so much and why he felt abandoned when she went out. He realized his father had felt abandoned by his mother, who had died early in their marriage. He had taken his father's feelings of abandonment as his own and was trying to prevent the same circumstance from occurring in his life. Yet, his effort to protect himself was creating more distance between his wife and himself—the very thing he didn't want to happen. As he stopped making her wrong and became more loving and accepting, he realized that she was very loyal and was not going to abandon him. Their relationship became calmer and more loving as he let go of needing her to stay around constantly and trusted that everything she did honored both of them.

You can choose peace
no matter how others are acting.

When you have unhappy emotions, don't think another person caused them. If you are angry, stop blaming another person for making you angry. Instead, work directly with your feelings of anger. Learning about why you are feeling angry will do more to take you higher than trying to figure out how to get the other person to change.

Waiting for others to act in certain ways to be happy is making your happiness dependent upon something outside of yourself. It is turning your power over to other people and allowing them to determine how you feel. Calm emotions come from knowing that what you feel is your choice. You do not want your good feelings to depend upon another person or an outside situation. Put your energy and time into going higher and making your own life work.

Spiritual growth involves developing the ability to understand yourself and to act in higher and higher ways. Everything in your life is teaching you about yourself. Do not make yourself wrong if you have a lot of turbulence in your life; see it as an opportunity to grow and know more about yourself.

Notice that you have already gained a level of mastery over your emotions, for there are certain situations that might have greatly upset you years ago that you now let pass quickly. Perhaps when someone slighted you in the past you felt bad about it for days. Now you simply shrug and decide it's their problem, not yours. You will get to a point, if you aren't there already, at which you can say, "People are the way they are, and I will not take their actions personally. In fact, their negative behavior is showing me that they need my love even more."

The higher your consciousness, the more your emotions will affect others, even if they are not physically near you. Everyone sends out an emotional broadcast. As your vibration increases, you have more life-force energy pouring through you and your broadcast affects more people. As you grow you have more and more responsibility to send out a peaceful and harmonious broadcast. In the higher dimensions, where all are telepathically linked as one consciousness, it is important that everyone contribute high, harmonious feelings to the whole. You may have noticed how one very upset person can affect a whole roomful of people, and how one very powerful, wise, and loving person can set a high tone that everyone follows.

> All *negative emotions show you*
> *where you are not aligned*
> *with the vision of your Higher Self.*

If you are in emotional crisis or turmoil, do whatever is nurturing to you. Curl up with a book, take a warm shower, or buy something special for yourself. Make space in your room to sit and think, read, or listen to music. Do something for yourself that makes your environment more beautiful or elegant. It is a time to love yourself. Nurture yourself in small ways, for as you do you will learn to nurture yourself in bigger ways. Love yourself and all your emotions as they come up. Take the time to examine what positive things you are learning from this turmoil. Remember that crises offer opportunities to reach the deepest level of your being and know your Higher Self in new ways; often that is why you create them.

You can change and release your emotions more rapidly by thoroughly experiencing them when they appear. Feel the emotion in your body. Where is it located? If it had a color, what color would it be? Don't try to talk yourself out of the feeling; let yourself feel it. After you have identified it in your body, send light to that area. You will discover that most emotions, even the strongest ones, pass quickly after you experience them, love them, and hear their messages. Stop thinking about whatever problem is creating the strong emotion, and focus on the feeling of the emotion itself. Breathe deeply and imagine your body being filled with light.

As you thoroughly feel your emotion, you can release it. After releasing it, feel the higher side of that emotion. Every negative emotion has a positive emotion on the other side. Ask for the positive emotion to now come in and replace the negative one you felt.

Music can have a very soothing effect on your emotions. Both vibrate and have resonance and rhythm. You may have noticed that when you put on beautiful music or environmental sounds it calms you or makes you feel more joyful. Use music as a tool to feel calm or however else you want to feel.

You can also change your emotions through meditation and quieting your mind. Certain thoughts trigger certain emotions. As you think calmly, you calm your emotions. Your emotions also respond to actions of your physical body, and they can be affected by certain foods. Many forms of exercise, such as walking, running, swimming, and bicycling, are calming to the emotional body. They quiet the mind and bring your thoughts up to a higher vibration by creating a smoother flow of energy.

You can choose peace over worry, calm over turbulence, and love over conflict. As you follow and listen to the guidance of your Higher Self your life will work in easier, more joyful ways. As you calm your emotions, you become more transparent to the turbulence of the earth plane and will transform it to the smooth, harmonious, and finer vibrations of your Higher Self.

Calming Your Emotions

MEDITATION

The purpose of this meditation is to attune your emotions with the pure, high, fine feeling-tones that exist in the higher dimensions.

Steps: Get into your Higher Self state for this meditation.

1. You can use your breathing to influence your emotions. Start by breathing deeply, exhaling so that you push out even more air than normal. As you inhale, straighten your spine and adjust the back of your neck and head so that your energy can flow up your spine and out through the top of your head.

2. Imagine you are in a cocoon of light, and you are floating upward into the higher dimensions. In these dimensions, there are actual places where beautiful energy-tones, notes of the purest emotions, emit their guiding vibrations. Each place emits a different vibration of the purest quality. Some vibrations are feeling-tones of love, compassion, courage, harmony, joy, or peace. There are places with vibrations for every beautiful feeling you can imagine. These pure vibrations are like tuning forks, providing reference tones to make these higher vibrations available to all beings.

3. What feeling, such as confidence, love, or courage, would most benefit your growth right now? Think of this quality. As you do, you are drawn to the place where this feeling-tone exists in its purest note and strength. Sit in

this beautiful feeling-tone of whatever feeling you have chosen.

4. Let the broadcast being emitted from this place produce resonance in your emotions so that you take on this quality as your own. Feel yourself changing at a vibrational level.

5. Imagine yourself in a future situation, demonstrating this quality or feeling. In this future situation, you might feel the vibration of this pure quality pouring through you and becoming a part of you.

6. When you are ready, return to the room in your cocoon of light. You can return to this or any other feeling-tone at any time you want.

10

Allowing Your Higher Good

Your Higher Self is always leading you to your higher good. Your Higher Self loves you and wants you to have every good thing you can allow into your life. Think of how it feels to give love to a small child or a favorite pet. They allow you to love them without feeling they must give you something in return. You feel good and grow from being able to give to them. It is the same with your Higher Self—It wants to give you every good thing you can imagine, and even more than that!

Learn to receive all the good things your Higher Self has to give you.

Many of you need to learn how to receive. Most of you have received less than two percent of the good things your Higher Self can give you. Close your eyes for a moment and imagine the other ninety-eight percent coming to you. How does it feel?

Do you find yourself opening to receive it, or do you start limiting how much you can let in? Imagine yourself receiving even more, as if you were turning on a faucet and letting even more good flow to you.

You deserve to have a wonderful life filled with love, abundance, good friends, excellent health, and loving relationships. Your Higher Self is completely abundant, and as you open to your higher good you are aligning with your Higher Self. Start by believing that a good life is naturally yours, not something you have to earn or pay for. It is the higher plan of the universe for all beings to have lives of beauty, harmony, and abundance.

The principle of allowing is very important. You allow things into your life easily and effortlessly all the time. There are many things you think you deserve, and you do not think twice about having them. For instance, you may have all the food you want, good friends, respect and support from others, and many creative ideas. You can increase the good you bring into your life by learning how to allow yourself to have what you want.

Although you easily allow abundance into some areas of your life, there are other things you think you do not deserve or must work hard for. You deserve the greatest things you can imagine just as much as you deserve all the smaller things you so easily allow into your life. You do not have to do anything to "deserve" your higher good. You are a good and worthy person. People who have abundance, loving relationships, and happiness are not more deserving or better than you. They simply allow more good things to come into their lives.

You can allow things into your life more easily when you let any form work. For instance, instead of asking that a specific person love you, simply ask for more love, and allow it to come in all the ways and forms it can. It may come from your friends, children, or even strangers. As you allow more love into your life from all sources, you may find that the person you want to give you more love also becomes more loving.

Instead of thinking that you have to work to get things, see everything good that comes as something you "allowed" and gave permission to come into your life. You loved yourself enough to have it. Think of some of the good things you easily allow into your life right now. Give yourself a moment of appreciation for being able to allow your higher good in these areas. If every night you mentally made a list of all the good things you allowed into your life that day, you would more easily learn how to allow even more good things into your life.

As you grow spiritually, many good things will come to you. Your ability to accept them will accelerate your growth. You don't have to struggle; you can allow your higher good to flow easily into your life. Everything that happens can serve you and bring you joy.

Say to yourself,
"I now allow more good things into my life."

If something is going well and you find yourself saying, "Things are too good to be true—I wonder how long this will last," STOP! Instead, challenge yourself to imagine things getting even better. Think of something that is working well in your life right now. Make a mental picture of it becoming even better.

Your thoughts create your reality, so pay attention to any limited thinking. Learn to stop listening to those thoughts that tell you that you can't have what you want. You need to be observant to catch them when they come up, for you do not want them sliding by unnoticed.

One woman was dreading working on an upcoming project. She caught herself saying to her friends how hard and difficult the project would be. She decided to make a mental picture of the project being easy and turning out well. She pictured herself telling her friends after she finished the project how easily she had done it. To her surprise, the project WAS easy, and she did end up telling her friends how well everything went.

Is there something you are speaking of or thinking will be a struggle for you? Stop for a moment and imagine it working easily and well. What you picture is what you create, so picture the best outcome you can imagine.

You can have a life that works perfectly. You don't need to accept problems and crises as a way of life. Let go of the worries, struggles, and problems in your life. Simply allow them to leave. Give them permission to go. Eliminate the word "trying" from your vocabulary, for it invites more struggle. Instead of saying "I am *trying* to do this well," say "I *am* doing this well."

Everything happens for your higher good; the universe works in perfect ways.

Every situation is an opportunity to grow; everything that happens is giving you the opportunity to become stronger, wiser, and more loving. Everything that happens to you is for your higher good. Some situations offer you the opportunity to release an attachment or let go of an emotion that no longer serves you. Allowing your higher good means knowing deep inside that you are safe and loved and that your Higher Self is always working for you.

Start now to tell yourself that the universe is perfect and that everything you do and everything that happens to you is perfect. As you grow spiritually, you will gain a greater understanding of why things are happening, and you will come to see the perfection in everything that occurs. From the higher perspective of today, you may be able to look back into the past and know that things you once interpreted as negative offered you growth and new beginnings.

Trust that what other people do will in some way be for your higher good, even if you don't understand why. No matter what happens, tell yourself the universe is perfect, and everything that happens is perfect. If something you were hoping for doesn't happen, know that something even better will. Don't try to force your Higher Self to create your pictures of how things ought to be; know that a higher wisdom is always operating. Remember that your Higher Self is always giving you as much good as you will allow into your life.

If you have taken all the actions you have the inner guidance to take, surrender your need to be in charge and in control every minute. Your intellect wants to plan everything to turn out a certain way; it wants to be captain of the ship. Although it is fine to set goals, trust your Higher Self to bring you the essence of everything you want at the perfect time and in the perfect way. Your Higher Self is the real "captain," and It always puts you in perfect circumstances.

It takes a lot of energy to try to make the world work in the way your intellect thinks it should work. Put down the burden of trying to plan every small detail. You don't have to hang on tightly and watch over everything every minute to make sure nothing goes wrong. Simply pay attention, act on any inner messages you are receiving, and stay in the higher flow. Things will turn out better than you even imagined.

You can allow more good into your life by giving good things to other people. Whatever you give comes back to you multiplied. Give a smile, love, and good energy wherever you go. Give whatever you want to receive. Give it freely, not with the intent to get something back. If you want more love, give love. If you want more respect or support, give that to others, and you will find it coming back to you.

Allow people to give to you.

Are you truly open to receive love and good things from other people? Allow people to love you. Receive their love in all the ways they give it to you. People give you love in the ways they want to receive it; their giving may not always match your picture of what you want. Learn to recognize love in all the ways it is being given. One woman wanted her husband to stay home with her every night, and when he didn't she felt he didn't love her. He often put in late hours at work and was baffled by her thinking he didn't love her. In his mind, his working long hours was his gift to her, building a solid future for them and making sure their life worked in practical ways. She learned to recognize that his hard work was an expression of his love. She realized that he did love her, but he expressed it a different way than she expected.

Open to receive and believe you deserve even more than you can imagine yourself having. If you received a check for an enormous sum of money from a friend who wanted to give to you, would you accept it freely? Or would you look for hidden strings? Imagine now that this friend has unlimited wealth and wants to give to you because he or she loves you, and there are no strings attached. Would you accept it? Think of your Higher Self as your loving friend of infinite wealth, waiting to give you everything you are open to receiving. Spiritual growth, love, joy, and abundance are all waiting for you to accept them into your life.

You needn't feel guilty about receiving everything you want, having your life work, and being happy. Open to receive; know that as you do you are not taking from others, for other people's Higher Selves are willing to give to them too—as much as they can allow into their lives. Believe that unlimited abundance exists for everyone, for it does. It is waiting only for them to claim it and give it permission to come into their lives.

Allow people to be any way they want to be.

Give all the people in your life permission to be who they are. As you do, you increase your ability to love and accept yourself just as you are. As you accept and love yourself, you raise your vibration and attract more good into your life. Accept the things you can't change, and look for the good in them. For example, if you take a vacation and it rains the whole time when you have planned on sunshine, look for the gifts in the new conditions. Rather than bemoaning your bad luck, appreciate all the good things that the rainy weather and the changes it creates in your schedule give you. Your Higher Self led you to this experience for a reason. Affirm that the universe is perfect, even if you don't understand why things happen at the time.

Your Higher Self loves you and wants to give you true happiness, deep inner joy, and all the love you can imagine. Acknowledge every time you receive something, knowing that you deserve to have it and you have allowed it to come. As you learn to allow small things into your life, you can learn to allow bigger things as well, such as your spiritual growth and a life filled with laughter, abundance, and love. The more you open to the feelings of allowing and deserving, the more rapidly you will grow and be your Higher Self.

Allowing Your Higher Good

MEDITATION

The purpose of this meditation is to increase your ability to receive love and energy from the universe and your Higher Self and to be able to imagine every area of your life working perfectly.

Steps:

1. Sit quietly, take a deep breath, and imagine you are opening your heart to allow good things into your life. Think of something you easily receive into your life. Observe the feeling of receiving on as many levels as you can. How does your body feel when you receive? Does your breathing or posture change? How do you feel emotionally? Can you enhance this feeling of receiving?

2. Staying with this feeling of receiving, mentally invite and give permission for good things to come to you. Imagine yourself receiving all the good things your Higher Self has for you. Notice how much you can receive and let yourself open to receive even more. Open to new thoughts, more harmonious emotions, physical energy, and abundance in every area of your life. As you do you become one with the abundance of your Higher Self.

3. As you draw in these good things, imagine you are creating space—mentally, emotionally, and physically—for them. All you need do is imagine you are opening up the energy around you to create room for these good things when they come.

4. Imagine your Higher Self is handing you a silver chalice filled with life-force energy and complete abundance. When you are ready to have more in your life, drink from it. Fill yourself with as much abundance and energy as you can receive. As you come back to the room, feel yourself opening to receive even more good things, and affirm that you are ready to have them.

11

Accelerating Your Growth

Get quiet for a moment and ask yourself, "How long do I think it will take until I am enlightened?" Do you find yourself answering, "I never will," or, "It will take lifetimes"? Do you think it is presumptuous to imagine you could reach enlightenment in this lifetime and be your Higher Self all the time? You create your own reality, and it is possible to create the reality in which you achieve enlightenment in this lifetime.

You CAN become enlightened in this lifetime.

You may have heard that it requires lifetimes to achieve enlightenment and become your Higher Self. In times past it often did. The denser energies of your physical plane, the level of consciousness of humanity, and the small number of spiritual teachers made enlightenment available to only a few people with years of special training. It took much discipline and self-awareness to break through the dense earth energies, for the way had been opened by only a few people. Today, the wave of light that is moving through your universe and the high levels of consciousness that many people are reaching is opening a larger channel to the higher realms and creating opportunities for many thousands to reach enlightenment in this lifetime.

Your Higher Self is always growing, exploring, learning, and discovering new aspects of itself. Growing—reaching new levels of understanding, self-awareness, and aliveness—is one of the main goals of all life. Growth never ends, for even when you reach higher levels there are still further levels to go. Without growth there is a contraction of life-force energy. With growth you feel vibrant, alive, healthy, and joyful.

One of the most important elements in reaching enlightenment is the intensity of your desire to grow. The more you want to grow with all your being the more rapidly you will reach enlightenment. One spiritual master held his student under water until he gasped for breath. "You must desire enlightenment as intently as you just wanted air—and then you will have it just as quickly," he told the student as he released him. This is a popular story because it illustrates so well the relationship between the desire for your spiritual growth and its attainment.

You may have heard that to desire anything is wrong. Yet, your desires teach you many things about yourself and the nature of reality. If you desire things that cause you suffering, that suffering will teach you to desire things that bring you joy.

Even fulfilling material desires can create spiritual growth. Behind the desire for a new home or car is the desire to grow, expressed in a familiar form. As you gain mastery over manifesting your material desires, you will come to realize that material objects, prestige, fame, and wealth have little value unless they serve your higher purpose. You will reach a point where you have an increasingly strong desire to be your Higher Self. For some, that desire may come from fulfilling other desires and learning which desires truly serve them and which ones do not.

How much do you desire growth? To intensify your desire to grow, ask your Higher Self to show you how your life will become even better as you grow spiritually. Some people think that growing spiritually means you have to give up all the things you love doing. Instead, imagine that the more you grow the more joyful and peaceful your life will become. You will be even more in touch with the stable, balanced, and calm inner part of yourself. You will be doing things you love and carrying out your higher purpose with a sense of deep inner satisfaction.

At a certain level of evolution desire disappears and you just *are*. You don't desire, you don't want anything, and you are not in a state of having and not-having. Until you reach that level, use desire as the tool it is. You have desire for a reason—so that you can desire your spiritual growth and thus be your Higher Self. Want your growth so much that it becomes an all-pervasive thought, for the more you desire it, the more you bring a spiritual orientation to everything you do, and the more rapidly you reach enlightenment.

If you want to grow, it is important to examine your beliefs about growth. You will want to have flexible beliefs, an open mind, and trust that the universe is friendly. Do you believe that growth is a struggle, that it comes out of pain and crisis, that it takes a long time, or that it will probably take more than this lifetime for you to become your Higher Self? By choosing to hold positive thoughts about growth you can expand your potential for evolution. Growth can come instantaneously, you can grow with joy, and you can reach enlightenment in this lifetime.

You can grow with joy rather than struggle.

If you believe that growth comes from struggle, you will create crises by which to grow. One of the greatest gifts you can give yourself is to dissolve any negative pictures you have about growth. Give yourself permission to have valuable and worthwhile things, such as your spiritual growth, come easily. It takes far less time and energy to grow through joy than to grow through struggle.

Some people enjoy telling stories of how hard something was for them, as if their struggle was an accomplishment. How much more fun it would be to trade stories about how easily things came! You do not have to work hard day and night, feel exhausted, or surmount incredible odds and obstacles to have worthwhile achievements and grow spiritually.

Some of you worry when things get "too easy." As you increase your vibration things *will* get easier. The challenge lies not in how hard things are, but in how expansive you can make your vision and how much can be accomplished with economy of energy, joy, and creative intent.

If you have a situation in your life right now that is less joyful than you want it to be, realize that it is teaching you important lessons. If you are in a crisis you may be reaching inward to the deepest part of your being and gaining a new strength and courage. You can choose to learn these lessons and gain these qualities with joy. Simply stop for a moment and make the decision to do so. Things may not change overnight, but they will change. Your Higher Self will begin to create circumstances that allow you to experience the same growth through joy that in the past you created through struggle.

You can grow instantaneously.

Spiritual growth does not have to be a step-by-step process; it can be instantaneous. Think of some quality you would like to have right now, such as inner peace, greater focus, or more self-love. How long do you think it will take for you to acquire it? You do not have to wait a year, five years, or a lifetime. You can increase your experience of this quality right now. Say to yourself, "I accept more of this quality into my life. I am now more peaceful, focused, and loving to myself," or whatever fits the quality you choose. As you say these affirmations you increase your experience of these qualities.

When you say affirmations, it is important to say them in the present tense. Rather than saying, "I will be peaceful," which puts it off to a future time, say instead, "I am now peaceful." Your subconscious mind does not know the difference between what is true and what you think is true. As you say these statements you are reprogramming your subconscious mind to accept these thoughts as your reality. As it does it will create changes in your life to match this new inner reality.

Making your everyday life work is an important part of spiritual growth.

Paying your rent, taking good care of yourself, and being self-sufficient are as important to your spiritual growth as meditating. Growth for most of you comes from living life fully, not from avoiding life and going off to a cave to meditate all day. You are here to learn from each person, each situation, and every challenge you have. You are here to learn to be fully present and aware of what is happening around you, adding more clarity, harmony, and light to all you do.

Spiritual growth is learning to make your life work in every area, from your relationships to your career. As you put your spiritual light into everything you do, bring awareness and love to all your activities, and turn every experience into an opportunity for growth, you are being your Higher Self.

In the beginning your spiritual growth may be something you focus on only occasionally. As you continue on your path, it will become an increasingly important part of your life.

You will begin to turn everything you do into an opportunity to grow spiritually, even your everyday activities. Washing dishes, driving to work, or other routine things can provide you with an opportunity to grow. Can you be totally in the moment, focusing all your attention on what you are doing? Can you observe your thoughts from a new, higher level and change them into even more positive, uplifting ones? Can you keep your mind on one thing at a time, or send out love through your heart to the people around you? Every single activity you do, no matter how mundane, presents the opportunity for you to do it in a higher state of consciousness.

You are not far from being enlightened just because you can't keep your heart open all the time, remain in a state of constant bliss, or meditate all day. As your personality comes increasingly under the influence of your Higher Self, there will be many moments when the connection is weaker and many when it is stronger. Old fears and concerns may surface. Look at how long these difficult moments last. As you grow you will move through these states more and more rapidly. You will have more frequent feelings of clarity, purpose, and direction; your ability to nurture yourself and serve others will increase.

At first there may be little evidence of your spiritual progress. As time goes on, your ability to return to and stay in a higher state of consciousness will increase. Your insights will become more numerous. Coincidences, telepathic connections, and flashes of inner knowing will occur more often. Acknowledge these moments, for as you do you will draw more of these events to you.

Accelerating your growth also comes from accepting and loving yourself as you are right now. Some of you think that you will love yourself better when you have become evolved and perfect. Many of you are too critical and hard on yourselves. Spiritual growth comes from loving yourself as you are now, not from making yourself wrong because you haven't reached some imaginary ideal of perfection. You are perfect as you are now. Start finding the good in yourself more often. Appreciate all the things you do well, and acknowledge all the moments you really do like yourself. Make yourself right rather than wrong. Spiritual growth is not something you work hard for. It comes from staying with your process, realizing that everything that happens to you is part of your spiritual growth.

Each shift to a higher consciousness makes the next shift easier.

The closer you get to enlightenment the more often you see signs of your progress. You may spend years laying a foundation and then suddenly leap forward in many areas at once. It may take years for some people to make the decision to grow and to take their first steps, but the time between successive shifts will grow shorter and shorter.

One reason your growth accelerates is that at a certain level you gain the tools to start taking charge of your own growth. In the beginning, you are less conscious of what to do to direct your growth. At this stage, the opening of your energy centers comes through your service to others and your daily learning experiences. Much of your learning is done first through the personality, which comes increasingly under the guidance of the Higher Self.

At a certain level of growth, you begin directing the opening of your energy centers. This accelerates your growth because your energy centers change your personality more rapidly than working directly on your personality. Many of you are approaching this level right now as you work on your energy centers and your emotional, mental, and spiritual bodies through meditation and other techniques.

One of the greatest challenges to your growth can be your personality, which can feel threatened by the increasing role your Higher Self plays in your life. Your personality may try anything it can to get you to stop growing, particularly after you have taken a big leap forward in some area. It may tell you to protect yourself or give you many reasons why you shouldn't continue moving ahead. Some of its methods include anger, depression, emotional swings, and simply not feeling like yourself.

If you have listened to the peaceful voice of your Higher Self and you get a sense that it is all right to continue with this particular path of growth, send love to the feelings you are having, and tell your personality that you intend to go forward. Ask for its cooperation, and tell your personality it will experience an even more wonderful world as you become your Higher Self.

Your accelerated growth means that you are making a new and deeper connection to your Higher Self. This can sometimes create a release of old patterns. Often when you take a leap forward the pattern that was holding you back the most may surface. Don't blame outside circumstances for the way you feel; look within and ask yourself what pattern or belief you are being shown. Ask your Higher Self for guidance about how you can release this pattern.

The issues that come up for you are showing you the most important patterns to work on to accelerate your growth. Love and appreciate them for all the gifts they offer you. Remember that every pattern or event that happens provides you with the opportunity to act in the highest way you have ever acted and occurs to bring out the best in you.

Give yourself the gift of growth; do not give away your power by waiting for someone else to help you grow. Some of you say, "If only my mate, friend, parents, or children would become more spiritual, if only they would meditate with me, eat healthier food, and always act kind, then I could be a more spiritual person." Do not wait for others to become more spiritual so that it will be easier for you. You are the leaders and teachers; make your behavior an example. Say things like, "I will meditate at night; I will be calm, loving, and confident," or, "I will learn this new skill; I will take walks in the woods, get fit, or change my diet. My partner does not need to cooperate for me to begin."

*You*r *spiritual growth*
is the greatest contribution
you can make to yourself.

As you grow spiritually, you will gain many tools to create
real results in the physical world. Your spiritual growth will
contribute to your mastery of living, allowing you to live with
more joy, aliveness, and love. Any energy you spend on growth
will come back to you multiplied. The more you work on your
spiritual growth, the more easily you will manifest what you
want. Every moment spent loving others, growing, and expressing your aliveness will create enormous gains.

Stop for a moment and make a commitment to your growth.
Mentally say, "I now commit to my spiritual growth and make
it a priority." Think of spiritual growth as a great gift to yourself, a wonderful treat you now deserve to have. Believe you
can be your Higher Self and reach enlightenment in this lifetime—and you will!

Accelerating Your Growth

MEDITATION

The purpose of this meditation is to program at a cellular level an acceleration of your growth. This will assist you in shifting your beliefs to enable you to reach your highest potential in this lifetime.

As you program at a cellular level, the pictures you send to your DNA can change your vibration, your magnetism, your aura, and your life.

Steps: Get into your Higher Self state for this meditation.

1. Picture yourself growing smaller and smaller, taking your consciousness, like a point of light, to the very core of all the cells in your body.

2. You are now a dot of light traveling into the center of the nucleus of your cells. You can be in one of them or all of them at once. In the nucleus of your cells is your DNA, which contain your life code.

3. Ask your DNA to release any programs, decisions, or beliefs that are not serving you and your growth. You do not need to know what these beliefs are; simply ask for them to be released.

4. Send love through your heart to all your DNA. Surround your DNA with light.

5. Mentally tell your DNA that you want to reach your highest potential in this lifetime. Ask for its assistance to

bring in new programs, beliefs, and thoughts that will make it possible to reach your highest potential in this lifetime.

6. As you finish and return your awareness to the room, decide you will embrace every opportunity presented to you to grow. Affirm that you are ready to reach your highest potential in this lifetime. Make an even greater commitment to your spiritual growth. Start by loving and accepting yourself as you are right now, acknowledging the light, love, and power that you already have within you.

12

Choosing Your Reality: Creating Probable Futures

To grow spiritually it is important to know you create your own reality. A major turning point in your growth comes when you begin to take responsibility for everything that happens. When you realize that it is possible to create the life you want (even if you don't yet know how), you and your Higher Self become the captain of your ship.

You are the source, the creator of your life. You are the one who reaches upward, grows spiritually, and connects with your Higher Self. You create your reality through your thoughts, emotions, beliefs, and intent, which determine your vibration and thus the people, objects, events, and circumstances you attract to your life. Your emotions and your intent determine how fast you get what you are thinking about. Everything in your life comes from a thought or feeling you have, for your inner world of thoughts and feelings creates your outer world of events, objects, and relationships. Because you create your own reality, you can choose any reality you want.

Because there is a time lag between your thoughts and their appearance in your reality, some people do not yet realize they create their reality. Yet, you could trace every event that happens to people back to a thought, picture, belief, emotion, or intent they had at some point in their lives. Every decision and choice you make is shaping your reality.

> The growing belief that you
> create your own reality
> is one of the most major shifts
> happening right now.

Until recently, the existing mass belief has been that people are at the mercy of vast, uncontrollable forces. Many of your cultural and social structures are designed to protect you against these forces. The thought that you create your own reality is sweeping through the minds of millions. All those who are searching and awakening to their Higher Selves are becoming aware that they create their own reality. It is being shared in dream states and through each person's Higher Self.

Your positive thoughts and beliefs can make a contribution to others. As you believe that you create your own reality and take responsibility for your life, your telepathic broadcast of this goes out to others. Your thoughts that you create your own reality are assisting others in knowing this and taking control of their own lives. Your beliefs and positive pictures are added to the collective pool of consciousness and are then available for others to tap into as they grow.

Thoughts held in common by masses of people determine the way your world works. As more and more people understand that you create your own reality, many major changes will occur in your society. Understanding that the way you think affects the world you experience around you will create many positive changes in your society.

You have only begun to see the consequences of people taking responsibility for their lives. Believing that you create every experience as an opportunity to grow will change your legal system, your government, your schools, and even the products that people manufacture.

When people know they can create what they want and learn how to do it, they will feel more powerful and in control of their lives. As they learn more about the principles of creating their own reality, they will begin to have lives of increasing abundance, love, and spiritual growth. People must believe they have the ability to change their own reality for the better before they will believe they can assist in changing the world for the better.

You can live in the probable reality where there is a clean environment and humanity is at peace.

There are many probable futures for humanity. In one, people have become responsible about the environment, exist together in peace, and honor the earth and each other. If you imagine the world growing more beautiful, people choosing to be more loving to each other, and a clean environment, you will start moving into the probable universe where that happens. If you focus on the wonderful, positive aspects of the world and see the beauty and love in everyone, you will vibrate with and flow into a more positive reality.

There are many choices available about the kind of reality you can live in. You live in an age of opportunity and choice. Think of the choices available 200 years ago, and think of how many choices you have available now. New realities and the opportunities they offer exist now that didn't exist anywhere on the earth even 50 years ago. For instance, choices of being an aerospace engineer, working with computers, or acting on television didn't even exist as possibilities. There are millions of realities you can choose from right now. You can live a primitive life without modern technology, or you can live a life filled with telecommunication, cars, airplane travel, and computers.

If you imagine world peace, a gentle global climate, and a stable economy and earth, you will flow into the reality that matches your pictures. By picturing the world you would like to live in, you can become a part of the probable reality in which that occurs. Even if you don't encounter these things on a global scale, you will find your own world peaceful, your personal economy stable, and yourself living in a place with a gentle climate.

When you first begin picturing the probable universe you want to live in, such as a world of peace, love, and clean air, conditions will change in ways that seem logical and believable to you. You won't wake up one day and find everything different. If you make enough changes in your internal pictures, and believe that they can come true, you will eventually find yourself in the probable universe you are picturing.

There are probable realities where an earthquake or earth changes occur in your area, and probable realities where they do not. When psychics look into the future, they see the various probable realities for people focusing on that particular reality. Their predictions may be true for those who are vibrating with those probable realities and not true for those who aren't.

If you worry constantly about earthquakes and disasters, you may experience the probable reality in which they occur. Even if they don't happen on a major scale, you will be drawn to those places in the earth that are undergoing dramatic change. You can start vibrating with the reality you want to live in by imagining the best conditions you can. Instead of picturing things growing worse, picture things growing better. If you catch yourself worrying about the environment, weather, earth changes, or larger-scale events, imagine things turning out wonderfully.

Think of the earth as becoming more beautiful and believe that it is possible to live in a place with clean air and a healthy environment, and you will create it as true in your reality. You will be creating a positive vision that becomes telepathically available to others. When enough people hold a positive vision of the future, it will come about, for your thoughts and intent create your reality.

You can create any reality you want; there are no limits to what you can have.

You can create your personal reality any way you want. Right before you fall asleep is a powerful time to create a new reality. Think of the day ahead. Visualize your ideal day, and imagine yourself waking up full of energy. These thoughts will go out to the future and meet up with you the next day. Challenge yourself to imagine having even more abundance than in the past—more energy, good feelings, clarity and focus, self-love, and compassion for others. As you master creating your ideal day, start visualizing even larger things. Allow yourself to daydream and fantasize, feeling the joy and good feelings you will have when you create the reality you want. Even five minutes two or three times a week can create enormous changes in the reality you experience.

You can choose to live in the reality where your loved ones fulfill their potentials and become all they can be. You can vibrate with the reality in which they do this by loving and accepting them as they are, and simultaneously holding the thought of them growing and manifesting their potentials. If you picture people failing and letting you down, or your being disappointed in them, you will vibrate to the probable reality where that happens. This doesn't mean you can get them to act the way you want. Your pictures of their higher purpose and how they might act if they expressed their potential may be different from that reality. You can, however, live in a universe where your loved ones grow and expand by picturing them doing so.

As you create a vision of the reality you want, don't make yourself wrong for where you are now, but applaud each sign that the new reality you are choosing is coming into your life. When you first start picturing what you want, it usually takes time for the vision to change from energy into form and to appear in your life. It must come from the higher dimensions of the Universal Mind into your physical reality. As time goes on, you will increasingly experience the results of your new, unlimited thoughts.

You can change your reality by rewriting the past.

Another way to change your present reality and create the reality you want is to rewrite the past. Everything you have now is the result of a choice or decision you made. Each time you make an important decision, you determine what future you create for yourself. For instance, you may have quit your job and gone back to school. This gives you a different future than if you had continued your job and not gone back to school.

As you change your past in your mind, you change your vibration and begin to draw to yourself a new future. If you want to be abundant, create a picture of a past in which you were abundant. If you want to be smarter, more creative, mechanical, disciplined, or loved, imagine a past where you were. It doesn't matter if this was your "real" past; your subconscious mind doesn't know the difference. It will draw circumstances to you that match your imagined past.

For instance, one man did an age-regression meditation that took him back to his childhood to examine why he had a recurring pattern. It seemed that every time he got close to having a successful relationship, he would suddenly start doing things to sabotage and eventually end it. Because he was in a good relationship and didn't want the old pattern to assert itself again, he decided to look into the past for answers.

While reviewing the past, he saw himself as a child and realized that as he watched his parents fight one night, he had made a strong decision never to get married. This decision was still operating many years later! He mentally changed the past; he forgave his parents for fighting and rewrote the scene to see them acting kind and loving to each other. He mentally "erased" his earlier decision. This time, he did not sabotage his relationship; it grew richer and closer than any he had ever had.

What you accept as true will create your reality.

Choose what information and situations you agree with and want as your truth. What you accept as your truth will create your reality. If you read something you don't like or don't agree with, don't accept it; it isn't true for you. It may be true for others, but you don't have to make it part of your reality. Instead of accepting others' opinions of reality, say, "I choose my reality. Do I choose the reality I am hearing or reading about? Does it empower me, serve in practical ways to make my life better? Will believing this truth bring me joy, aliveness, and more love?"

You do not need to accept others' views of reality that are based on fear and scarcity; you do not need to prepare for a fearful future. Even if there is an economic crisis or earth up-heaval somewhere, these need not affect you. You can create your own personal economy of abundance by believing in abundance and choosing this as your reality. Your future can be one of love, laughter, and inner peace. You can create your own positive future and you can choose any reality you want.

Choosing Your Reality

MEDITATION

The purpose of this meditation is to create the reality of your awakened heart, where you live a life that is loving to you and your dreams come true.

Steps: Get into your Higher Self state for this meditation.

1. As your Higher Self, create a vision of your life as you would like it to be in several years. Let yourself feel the good feelings having this reality will give you. Start with your relationships by imagining all of them bringing you love and joy. Think of your job, financial situation, health, spiritual life, recreation, social activities, energy, life-style, and place you would live. What would you love to do during the day? Allow yourself to daydream and fanta- size about a life that is loving and nurturing to you. Picture the world as you would like it to be—such as a clean environment, a peaceful world, and so on. As you picture these things, you vibrate with the reality in which they happen.

2. After you have created a vision of your ideal life, imagine you are working with this vision as unmanifest energy as you did in the Universal Mind meditation on page 37. Create this higher probable reality as energy, making your ideal life into energy that is as beautiful, light-filled, and harmonious as you can imagine. You may want to make a symbol of it and play with the symbol.

3. Bring the energy of your highest probable future into your DNA. Let it change your frequency and vibration at a cellular level so that you are vibrating with this higher reality. Radiate this energy through your body, emotions, and mind.

4. Imagine several years have passed, and you are now your future self who lives in this higher probable reality. From the perspective of your future self, what is your life like? Describe your circumstances and how you feel. Speak of the future in present tense. For instance, say to yourself, "I now have _____ ," as you describe life as your future self.

5. As your future self, send energy back through time to assist you in getting to this reality even more easily. Ask your future self if it has a message for you.

6. When you are finished, slowly come back into the room, bringing a sense of this new reality with you.

13

Going Through the Void

The void is a state of consciousness you can go into to expand beyond your current limits, let go of old things, and move to your next level of growth. In the void you leave behind familiar structures, habits, thoughts, behaviors, and attitudes, and go deep within to create new ones that match your higher vibration. In this state you can receive insights and do much inner work. It can last for minutes, hours, days, or even months. You will experience the void throughout your spiritual journey. It is your ability to live near the void, go into it at will, and make it your friend that will assist you in growing even faster and with more joy.

Imagine a bird flying happily in a jetstream. It looks upward, and sees a higher flow that it wants to join. It begins to leave its familiar path and fly to the higher one. However, conditions between the two paths aren't certain. It may hit turbulence and fall below the original path temporarily. It may be carried way above the higher path or find that the space between has very little air flow, making normal flight more difficult. By leaving the familiar jetstream, the bird learns much about itself. It discovers more about flying and the conditions that can affect its flight. Eventually it is able to stabilize and fly easily in the higher flow. Its experience is similar to what you encounter when you are in the void.

The void occurs when you are letting go of an aspect of your personality self that no longer fits who you are becoming. It represents a new level of surrendering your personality to the guidance of your Higher Self; it is the birth of a new part of your Higher Self into this reality.

The void is a state of transition and change.

You will experience the void again and again as you grow. In this state you may feel that your life is changing rapidly, something new is coming, or your foundations are falling away, leaving you nothing solid to hang on to. You may feel like something is happening inside but not see any changes in your life yet. It is not a comfortable place for your personality, which likes things to be certain and secure.

The void can come when you are between projects, have just had your last child leave home, or have quit a job and do not yet know what to do next. One of your close friends may have left or you need to move or find a new home. It sometimes feels like you are entering a new world where the game is played differently and you don't yet know the rules.

Every void is marked by issues of the heart. You will find yourself asking deep questions, such as, "How can I love and accept myself more? Am I lovable? Who am I? Can I have what I want? What would I love to do with my life?" You may find that you feel softer and more loving toward others in this time of uncertainty. You are raising your vibration, expanding beyond your old habits and patterns.

The void can make you feel much less social than normal. If you have always been in relationships, you may find yourself living alone or without a primary relationship. You may feel more distant from your husband or wife, even while you feel increased compassion and love for him or her. In the void you may have less desire than usual for intimate physical contact, which intertwines your aura with another's. During the time of the void you are clearing your aura of other people's energy as part of the process of raising your vibration.

You may feel empty or lonely inside even when surrounded by people. You may want more time alone. The desire to be alone, even feelings of loneliness, are reflections of your deepening desire to connect with your Higher Self. In your deeper wisdom, you know that your connection to others is not a substitute for a deeper connection to your Higher Self. As you spend time alone, you get to know yourself better. It is a time to know your feelings and thoughts, to think about what you want to do with your life. As you begin to know and make friends with yourself, your feelings of loneliness decrease.

You may feel physically different—over-energized or wanting to sleep more than usual. Sleep provides time for inner work to take place, and you may need more sleep to integrate all the internal changes that are going on. Some people worry because they have less energy than normal and can't explain why. If you don't honor the need for rest, you may find yourself getting minor illnesses to keep you quiet. Some people create back pain or various physical injuries that require them to take time off from their work and give them time to rest and think.

In the process of raising your vibration, you sometimes pass through a period of confusion. In the void the new is not yet established and the old hasn't yet left; they exist side by side. This can create confusion until you sort things out.

Your moods may be inconsistent. You may feel more emotional than usual, or feel very little emotion about anything. As your internal work grows more intense, your mind may feel different. The void is a time when you are learning to think in new ways. Because of this, it may be harder to think in the old ways. You might have moments when you have trouble thinking clearly, or you may forget things you knew the day before.

You may wonder if you are losing your memory. You may have more trouble than usual making quick decisions or knowing what you want. Yet, there will be periods of great clarity with new insights and ideas pouring through. You may even have times when you remember long-forgotten events from your past.

In the void your thoughts may be different than usual, as if you are measuring things by a new standard. It is as if you are shining a powerful light on your life and seeing things in a new way. You may be examining everything in your life, deciding what to keep and what to let go of. You may even feel that things are falling apart or that things you took for granted aren't working the way they used to. There comes a time when the vision of where you want to be requires you to let go of something you created. The void teaches you about your attachments. It is a time of examining your relationships, feelings, attitudes, and values, replacing those that no longer serve you with ones that do.

Not-knowing can be the doorway to true knowing.

The void is a time of not-knowing. It may feel like a state of not-doing, of nothingness. It is only when you stop knowing in your normal way and experience not-knowing that you can connect with new knowledge. This state of nothingness and not-knowing is a state of being rather than doing, of stillness and silence. Many of you fear the void because it offers neither a solid foundation nor a clear identity. What you have identified with may be changing to allow you to grow into a greater identity.

Allow yourself to go into the void for a few minutes each day by silencing your mind. Let yourself explore the nothingness. Silence is the doorway to greater knowing, and you will discover a richness of energy beyond description rather than "nothing." Each time you go into the void you will come out at a higher level.

The void gives you many choices and new possibilities.

As your connection to your Higher Self grows stronger, you draw to yourself many new opportunities that match your higher vibration. When you are in the void, any decision you make will have far-reaching effects, for you are at the intersection of many probable futures. Let go of all your preconceived ideas and explore your expanded range of choices.

Take time to fantasize and daydream. You may find yourself thinking of the future often and of how things could be different. Even if you can see no way yet to create the life you want, continue to imagine your ideal life. Your visions are creating the future, and you will draw to yourself the circumstances to bring about your visions.

As you raise your vibration, you will probably find yourself in the void more and more often. You can be experiencing the void in one area of your life and not others. For instance, your job might be quite stable and certain while your relationship with someone may be undergoing a big change.

If you are experiencing the void in any area of your life, be loving to yourself. Don't worry if no direction has yet revealed itself. You are raising your vibration rapidly in this area, doing much inner work, and opening your heart to love yourself more. As you do, new circumstances will start appearing that are better than what you had in the past. Love and accept your present circumstances too, for loving where you are will let you reach your new vision more quickly.

There is always a turning point while you are in the void. There comes a moment at which a deep inner note is sounded.

It is a note of determination, of stronger will, of a decision that will lead you in a new direction. There is a moment when a shift takes place, when you become clearer about what you want. Your self-love is greater, and you know within that you are ready to start creating what you want.

At first you may be only faintly aware of this new decision and what action to take to carry it out. Take the first steps that appear to you and the next steps will come. You then leave the void, the time of insights and new possibilities, and begin the stage of carrying out your insights. You are like the bird that has found the higher jetstream; you are flying in it and learning where it takes you.

One man found out that he had to move because the home he was renting was going to be put up for sale. He hadn't planned on moving and felt displaced. Then his closest friend took a job in another state and moved away. It felt like everything in his life was falling apart. At the same time he finished a large project—a book—on which he had been working and was wondering what to do next.

Instead of focusing on how uncomfortable he felt, he focused on the new opportunity he had to create better things. He began to view the uncertainty as having challenge and excitement in it, and he used this time to get clearer about what he wanted. He pictured himself living in a home that was even better than what he had and shortly found a wonderful place to live. He started meeting people and made several new friends whose company stimulated him. He stopped trying to think about what new book to write, and as he was relaxing one day an idea came to him that formed the basis for another book. As he left the void and moved into greater certainty, he began living a life that was much higher and more nurturing to him than the one he had before.

You don't have to wait for things to leave your life to use the opportunity present in the void. Whenever you feel an inner sense that things don't quite fit who you are any more, whenever you want to contemplate a new direction, simply get quiet and venture into the world of probable futures. Imagine living out different possible futures. Challenge yourself to think positively and expansively. Learn to love uncertainty and embrace the new.

Living in the void can be stimulating, challenging, and expansive.

Don't rush into a decision just to have things more fixed and secure once again. The universe works in perfect ways, and there are good reasons if things are changing. You can leave the void when you decide that you are ready and have made important inner choices. The void, with its lack of structure, certainty, and concrete direction assists you in taking major leaps forward.

As you come out of the void, you will find yourself wanting to reconnect with people, perhaps in new and more expansive ways. You will feel more certain about what you want and have a greater sense of purpose. As you leave the void, implementing your insights, you will see the positive results of your inner work begin to manifest.

Love the void, for even though nothing seems to be happening, it is a time when much inner work is being done. In the void you have the opportunity to create a new and higher future. Times of uncertainty are also times of new possibilities. Go for it—reach for the stars! Picture having everything you want. You may even find yourself learning to love the void for the opportunity it offers to take quantum leaps and accelerate your growth.

Going Through the Void

MEDITATION

The purpose of this meditation is to go into the void to expand beyond all previous limits and become the unlimited being you are.

Steps:

1. Take a deep breath, mentally relax your body, and start by imagining you are traveling through a tunnel. At the end of the tunnel is the void. As you start through the tunnel, you go past each of the colors of the rainbow. Feel each color as you are surrounded by it and notice its effects on your energy. These are beautiful, perfect colors. You travel through red, then orange, yellow, green, blue, indigo, and violet, in that order.

2. As you continue along the tunnel, you come to the end and go into the void. You have just left the color of violet; all colors are gone and you are passing through an area of no color. You are beginning to experience the nothingness of the void.

3. With "nothing" all around you, get a sense of your own energy. What is your energy like?

4. Let yourself and all of your energy systems fade and dissolve into this nothingness. Silence is all around you. See how long and with how much of your awareness you can sense this nothingness.

5. As you dissolve into the nothingness, imagine a wonderful thing is happening—you are becoming an enormous, infinite energy. Your boundaries are falling away and your energy is expanding at every level into the void. All possibilities exist for you in this void. Feel the richness of who you are. This is a place where anything and everything is possible. You experience yourself as an infinite being.

6. Now bring this expansive reality of the void back with you into your present reality. Imagine you are coming back into your current reality as a new person. You might symbolize this by seeing yourself as a beautiful butterfly emerging from your cocoon and spreading your wings, or as a flower unfolding its petals. You are charged with new possibilities, higher energy, and an expanded awareness of who you are.

14

Expanding and Contracting Time

Time is not as "real" and fixed as you might believe. Time is changing in the new energies that are coming. There are actually hours that pass slowly and hours that pass quickly. You may have noticed that some days seem very long and others seem very short. This isn't just your imagination or your perception; time is truly becoming more fluid and less fixed in the way it moves through your dimension.

In the higher dimensions, all that exists is the eternal NOW, the present moment of multidimensional time. When an idea is conceived, it is immediately complete from beginning to end. Events spread out from a central point, and you can experience any part of your idea by focusing your consciousness on that part. As you focus on the part you want to experience, you start existing in time, because you have taken a whole event and separated it into distinct parts. Time and space are what separate things. You can have many people in one space if they are separated by time, and you can have many people together at one time if they are separated by space.

Do *only those things that create*
your higher purpose
and you will have more time.

Your Higher Self experiences things as wholes and not as parts. It has an overview and sees every event from beginning to end. You can experience time as your Higher Self by experiencing things as wholes and not as their individual parts. You can do this by going as high as you can and viewing the larger picture of your life. You can do this with each project you are working on by having a vision and getting a sense of all the steps involved.

The more complete the picture and the higher your focus, the more you will know which activities are important to your higher vision and which are not. The time you save can be made available for other things. You may remember a time when you were able to get a more comprehensive view of something, and with that higher view recognized new actions you could take that would save you time and energy. That larger view may also have allowed you to let go of other activities that were no longer necessary.

If you want to get more done in less time, be aware of how what you are doing fits into the bigger picture of your life. Do this at every level. For instance, if you have a business, you would want to have a complete plan that coordinates sales with production, rather than letting each department work on its own. Otherwise, the sales department might sell more products than you could produce, or your production department might make products you couldn't sell. Both would have wasted a lot of time and not served the company in achieving its higher goals. If you had a plan and a higher vision, every department could work together to carry it out.

You not only want to be aware of the larger picture, you also want each part of your life to contribute to it and work together. When you focus on your spiritual growth and coordinate everything around that higher picture, you can contract time and grow "lifetimes" in a shorter period.

Before you take action, think about why you are doing something. Put it into the larger perspective of your life. Ask yourself, "How is this action accomplishing my higher purpose? Does it have to be done at this moment? Is there a higher way to do it?" As you put things into their larger perspective, you will be doing only those activities that serve your higher purpose.

Set aside a few moments to relax and think about the higher purpose of your life. Imagine you are your Higher Self giving yourself advice, and focus on your vision of your life and purpose. Ask what your higher purpose is in the next day, week, and month and how what you are doing right now fits into it. Mentally run through your upcoming day and sense which activities and which order of doing them feels good before you jump into action. A few moments spent putting things into a higher perspective may save not only hours each day, but even months of unnecessary actions.

The higher you go, the more you will see which activities you could eliminate, how things could be done more efficiently or differently, or how some things could be done by others. Don't take anything you do for granted. Don't think that something has to be done until you have thoroughly examined its purpose and how it fits into your higher purpose. This is one of the most important steps you can take to accelerate your growth.

**Follow your inner guidance
to get things done easily and joyfully.**

Following your inner guidance will give you more time as well as speed up time, for you will create things so quickly that you will have time left over to do other things. Your inner guidance will take you to whatever you want in the fastest way possible. If you are looking for ways to create your higher purpose through a job, you can go out, pound the pavement, knock on every door, and answer all the want ads. Or, you can create a vision of your perfect job; the skills you would like to use; the environment, pay, type of people, and hours that you want; and then take action only when you have the inner guidance to do so. If you do the latter your actions will produce the results you seek.

In this new wave of energy, you may be feeling that there aren't enough hours in the day to get everything done, that the demands on your time and life are increasing. Because time is no longer rigid and fixed, operating solely from an intellectual framework is going to make you feel more pressured. The more you try to do things logically, the more you make lists and force yourself to follow them, the more rushed you will feel. Although lists can help you focus, remain flexible and listen to your feelings.

It is important to follow your feelings and intuition, for they will put you in the higher flow of time. The new time is intuitive, not linear and sequential as in the past. You can no longer figure out when to do things solely by using logic and still be in the higher flow where things happen easily. Even though you make lists of things to do, your feelings may be telling you to do something else. Follow your feelings rather than your lists, and you will find them leading you to your goals in the highest, most efficient ways.

To have more time, slow down for a few minutes when you finish an activity. Before you go to another one ask yourself, "What do I feel like doing next? What would bring me joy?" Listen for the answers that you will receive. Sometimes the things you are drawn to do next won't appear logical or even productive. In the long run they may save you hours of work.

For example, your body may be telling you as you work that it would love to walk, stretch, or exercise. You think this is unproductive and that you should force yourself to work longer and ignore your body. However, you decide to honor your physical impulse and take a walk during lunch. That afternoon you get twice as much done as you normally do, and you have some important insights that save you hours of work. Trust your instincts and deeper impulses, for they lead you to do things in the fastest, most joyful ways.

If you follow your intuition, taking action only when it feels right, things will get done in much less time than you would expect, and you will be able to do far more than you can imagine. You flow with time when you stay in touch with your feelings and higher purpose. Intellectual time, which says, "Here is my list for the day; I must do things in this order," puts you in the position of doing things when that may not be in the higher flow.

One woman, who had been wanting a new job for weeks, got an inner message to go to her dentist for a checkup, so she made an appointment. She had been feeling guilty that she hadn't done more to look for her new job, but she hadn't had an inner sense of any action to take. While she was getting her teeth checked, her dentist told her of a friend who wanted to hire someone who had just her qualifications. She contacted his friend and easily got the job she had been wanting.

You are always directed to your higher good, even in the smallest ways. Have you ever had an urge to clean your house and then had a special, unexpected caller? Your Higher Self looks out over the universe, sees what is coming, and constantly broadcasts messages to you to assist you in being in the higher flow. Although the messages may be faint at first, the more you listen to and follow the messages you hear, the more messages you will receive and the clearer they will become.

The guidance you receive will lead you to more abundance, joy, and love. Your higher path will unfold more rapidly, and the timing of your projects will be just right. You will be one step ahead of people, ready with your work right as people are ready for it.

You can change time by being fully present and focused on what you are doing.

Time in your dimension is taking on many of the characteristics of time in the higher dimensions, where everything is simultaneous. Being in a higher state of consciousness when you do things allows you to use this new kind of time more effectively. Learn to be fully present, aware, and focused on what you are doing. You have probably experienced time standing still when you were doing something you loved. You were so absorbed in what you were doing you weren't even aware of time passing. You transcended physical, linear time and experienced the no-time of the higher dimensions.

Experiencing intuitive, multidimensional time involves becoming one with whatever you are doing, being so absorbed that you and what you are doing no longer have separate boundaries. It is as if you have extended your consciousness to what you are doing and it is now a part of you rather than something outside of you. Artists know this state in the moments when inspiration pours through them and time disappears. In this state, you can do hours' worth of work in minutes, for you have transcended your normal, linear time.

The way to have more time in this new wave of energy is to raise your vibration and handle things from a higher level. You do this by doing things only when you are in the right energy space to do them, when you can put your full attention on them. If you aren't in the right mood to do one thing, do something else you are in the mood to do. Trust that if you aren't in the mood to do something, there is something else that is more important to do at that moment.

When you aren't in the mood to do something, you are more separate from it. While you are doing it, you may be thinking of other things. When you are not one with what you are doing, you operate in linear, sequential time and things take longer.

Things that aren't done from a high level will usually be more work, may have to be redone or undone, and may create more time-consuming tasks in the future. Learn to be in the experience of what you are doing so thoroughly you are one with it as you do it, and you will be working with time as your Higher Self.

Many of you spend more time and energy worrying about doing things than doing them. How often have you put off doing something, thinking it might take too much work, only to find that once you were in the mood to do it and got started, it was easier than you thought? If there is something you keep putting off, let it go for a while and stop making yourself wrong for not doing it. Sometimes pressuring yourself to do something makes it harder to start.

To create more time, watch your words and thoughts about time. Do you say to yourself or others, "I never have enough time; I am so pressured, and I wonder how I'll get all this done"? Your words, thoughts, and beliefs are creating your reality, so begin by telling yourself you have all the time you need. Start saying such things as, "I have all the time I need; I do things in a relaxed, focused way." Even if you don't believe this at first, your words and thoughts will soon create this as your reality.

You can bring things into your life rapidly by imagining that you already have them.

You can learn to contract time and draw things to you more rapidly. Some of you want to create more abundance, attract your soul-mate, or lose weight more rapidly. Acting as if you already have something is very magnetic to bringing it into your life. For instance, you can accelerate your spiritual growth by pretending that you already have the qualities you are seeking. You might imagine already having the quality you want more of, such as peace or joy. If you want more abundance in some area, pretend you already have it. How would it feel? What would you do differently? Spend time visualizing anything you want, and imagine you already have it. Say to yourself, "I now have _____ , " filling in the blank with whatever it is you want to create. As you imagine having something, you become more magnetic to it and it comes into your life more rapidly.

To create things more rapidly, focus on the essence of what something will give you rather than its form. For instance, if you want a new car or home, focus on what you want to get out of having them. You may want a new car to give you reliability and a new home to give you more space, and so on. You can begin to create the essence of what you want right now. You can work with your existing car to make it more reliable; and perhaps you can clear out a corner of a room to create more space in your current home. By making your old car more reliable, you become more magnetic to a new, reliable car.

Ask what is the essence you expect to get from losing weight, having a new soul-mate, or whatever else you want. As you focus on the essence of what you want, you discover that there are many ways you can have the essence right now. When you bring the essence of what you want into your life, you become more magnetic to the specific form you want it to come in as well.

To your Higher Self, time is simply the number of steps that need to happen to have something occur. Think of what you want. Imagine going into the world of your Higher Self and seeing the whole of what you want to create, as if you can see it from beginning to end. Next, imagine you can sense all of the parts—the steps that need to be taken to create this. You don't need to know what the actual steps will be, just get a sense or imagine how many are involved.

Then speed things up by picturing yourself taking the steps more rapidly and joyfully. You might even see yourself skipping over steps and going directly to what you want. Loving yourself whether or not you have what you want and not "needing" something will assist you in taking the steps to bring it into your life more rapidly.

You can learn to change the way time works in your life, mastering the rate at which things happen. You can accelerate your growth and draw things to you more rapidly. You can learn to achieve a higher state of consciousness in which you become one with time, which will allow you to accomplish a great deal in your Higher Self's realm of no-time.

Expanding and Contracting Time

MEDITATION

The purpose of this meditation is to learn how to expand and contract time.

You may want a friend to ask you these questions, ask them mentally, or put them on tape and play them back, pausing to give yourself time to answer. If you are alone, you can answer these questions mentally, speak your answers out loud into a tape recorder, or write down your responses.

Steps: Get into your Higher Self state for this meditation.

Expanding Time. As your Higher Self, give yourself advice on the following questions. You might want to pretend your Higher Self is a wise consultant, advising you about these things.

1. What is your higher purpose for the next month? The next three months? The next year? Find out as much as you can about these higher purposes; state them in as many ways as possible.

2. What is the single most important thing you could do in each of these areas to accomplish your higher purpose:

    a. Livelihood (job, career, main activity).

    b. Material abundance (money, objects).

    c. Environment (living space, location).

    d. Spiritual growth activities.

e. Well-being (health/fitness, recreation, hobbies, travel).

f. Relationships. What are two of your most important relationships and what can you do to make a contribution to each of these people? How can these relationships contribute to your higher purpose?

3. Is there anything you might need to let go of to create this higher purpose? What level of commitment will it take to create it? How can you create this higher purpose with more joy?

4. What one step could you take in the next week to begin to accomplish this higher purpose?

Contracting Time. Think of your higher purpose for the next year. Imagine that there are a number of steps to create this higher purpose.

1. Get a sense of these steps, how many there are, how complex, what order they will occur in, and so on.

2. Picture yourself taking these steps joyfully, expanding and becoming lighter with each step. You might see yourself skipping over steps and going directly to your goal.

3. Let yourself feel the emotions you will have as if you have already created this higher purpose. Feel this increased radiance in your body. Say to yourself, "I have now created _____ (whatever your higher purpose is). "

4. When you are ready, return to the room, remembering all the guidance you have just received.

15

Becoming a Source of Light

You are the healers, teachers, and leaders. You are here to bring through new information, ideas, healing tools, and love to whatever areas you choose to work in. You will be working in many fields, for the new consciousness needs to be built in every area of society. As you grow spiritually and awaken your inner light, you will become a source of light and awakening for others.

You, as your Higher Self, existed in higher dimensions of light before you chose to be born. To live on this planet, your Higher Self first created a spiritual body, and this became the model that set up your chakras, meridians, and energy systems. Then your Higher Self drew to your spiritual body your mental, emotional, and physical energy bodies.

Imagine that one day you put on many layers of shirts, trousers, and socks, then added to those several heavy sweaters and overcoats. How would you feel? This is what it feels like for your Higher Self to come into a physical body. You wonder why you feel so heavy at times! When your spirit leaves your body, you shed this shell and return to the formless essence of your Higher Self.

Because you came from dimensions of greater spirit and light, many of you find it hard to live in the earth dimension of matter. Some of you haven't fully connected with your body yet and prefer to live in your mental world more than in the physical world. You may wish you could create things as quickly and easily as you can imagine them in your mind, for you have faint memories of the higher dimensions where you created things at the instant you thought of them.

As your Higher Self, you had a wide network of like-minded friends, all working together in higher purpose. Many of you came to the earth plane together as a soul-group. You may feel a moment of recognition for each other when you meet in your earth life—as if you are meeting an old friend you haven't seen for a while. Some of you have been working for many lifetimes upon the earth plane. Some have come only recently. You were drawn here because of the enormous opportunity these times offer to heal, teach, and bring light, which gives your Higher Self the opportunity to grow even more radiant.

Your Higher Self knew how much courage it would take to come into the dimensions of matter—the earth plane—with its greater turbulence and leave behind the fine, clear, harmonious energies of the higher dimensions. Your Higher Self wanted the growth that comes from learning to bring the finer energies of Itself into your earth life and the earth plane. Your Higher Self felt that the lessons you would learn by being in the more turbulent energies of the earth plane would greatly add to Its radiance as you learned to hold your light steadily amidst these energies.

Many of you still have faint memories of the constant love and support you had received in the higher dimensions. As a result, you may have had a difficult childhood at times, feeling misunderstood or unappreciated by those around you. You may have felt the world should make more sense and that people didn't need to feel the pain and confusion they experienced. You may have tried hard to please everyone around you, because you wanted others to feel good. You could "feel" others' emotions and often didn't know who you were since you became lost in their feelings. You may have even taken others' pains and burdens as your own and tried to solve their problems for them.

You may have chosen a difficult childhood because you knew it would build the strong character needed to accomplish your life purpose. When others don't recognize you for who you are, you have the opportunity to grow by believing in yourself without needing outside validation. This lack of outside validation helps you become more self-sufficient and independent, allowing you to find your own directions without relying on others. It makes you more aware of what others are experiencing and develops your compassion.

As a child, you were not totally alone and unrecognized. Your parents recognized who you were to the degree that they recognized who they were. Many high beings volunteered to come as teachers or put themselves around children so they could plant seeds of growth for you, the healers and teachers. You may remember a teacher or special adult friend who made a significant difference in your life.

Many high beings are mothers, fathers, schoolteachers, and caretakers of children, for many of the children being born today are evolved and old souls. Those special people who come to work with children know that a few words of encouragement, a moment of recognition, and a spark of interest can awaken the incoming children of light to their purposes and increase the effectiveness of their entire lives.

You knew how strong you would be inside and that no matter what difficult situation you found yourself in, you would find a way to transform it. The first order of business for all of you has been to heal yourselves, for most of you came into vibrations and energies that were much more turbulent than those you existed in before you were born. Don't make yourself wrong for feeling doubt, guilt, grief, or fear. Realize that these are the feelings that come with being in a physical body at this stage of mankind's evolution.

You may have chosen to personally experience some of the areas humanity as a whole has not yet evolved in—such as fear or doubt—knowing that the ways you find to change them in yourself will be tools you can give to others. For every part of yourself that you bring to a higher vibration, you make it easier for others to bring a similar part of themselves to a higher vibration. Your choices become telepathically and energetically available to others. Every time you love yourself or express compassion or wisdom you are making a contribution to all humanity.

You were aware that you would be coming to earth during a time when many changes were taking place; in fact, during your lifetime more significant changes will take place than during any other time in history. For instance, your population is increasing faster than at any time in the past, and your social structures and cultural structures will be changing rapidly to catch up with the changes this requires.

You are the builders of the new. You are here to assist people in making this transition, and you can start by expanding your own consciousness, healing yourself, and getting your life's work out to the world.

Times of turbulence, in which things are changing, offer much opportunity for growth. You might think of a bird trying to fly; if there is no current of air it is more difficult to take off. Like the bird, you need just the right amount of movement and change—turbulence—to grow. Many of you began more actively seeking your spiritual growth during times of crisis and change. Although you do not need crises to grow, many of you only make changes when things get stirred up or when the old is no longer working as well as it used to.

Since you were a child you may have felt you had a special purpose or mission.

You may have felt you had a special purpose, a mission to accomplish, though you probably did not know what it was. Your doubts about your worth may have increased as you found little outside validation of your inner sense of personal value. Yet, in spite of hardships or lack of support from others, you were pulled forward by a powerful inner force to keep seeking, finding, and fulfilling your greater purpose.

Because the density of matter can often block you from remembering who you are and what your higher purpose is, many of you have gotten lost in self-criticism and doubt. More of you have lost your effectiveness in carrying out your higher purpose through self-doubt and too much humility than for any other reasons. It is important to believe in your dreams; they are showing you your special purpose. If you haven't yet found your higher purpose, trust that everything you are doing is leading you to this higher path. You will have a greater awareness of what your special purpose is as you continue to grow.

Each of you was born with a special purpose, a unique role to play that no one else could fill. You have chosen to be at the forefront of the change that is coming, to contribute to building the new forms that will support a superconscious reality. Many of you are drawn to being self-employed so that you can freely design and implement your own ideas; if you work for a company, you prefer positions that allow you to have a say in how things are done.

You are ahead of your time.

You are the holders of the vision of what is possible for humanity to accomplish. You may have wondered why you think differently from others or why you sometimes feel like you don't fit in as well as others. Some of the thoughts and ideas you have that are now uncommon and unusual will be the thoughts that bring about the changes to higher consciousness in years to come. You may be drawn to areas such as ecology, the peace movement, science, technology, psychology, metaphysics, or others that contribute to a new vision for humanity.

Imagine you are walking up a mountain. There are many people in front of you and many people in back of you. Now imagine that the beings ahead of you turn around and send you lines of light, love, and energy, lighting up your path and making your journey easier. You see with increasing clarity where you are going. Your footsteps become more sure. You are able to climb even faster. Now imagine turning around and sending out your light and wisdom to those behind you, broadcasting encouragement and knowledge of the path you have just tread.

You do not need to make your spiritual journey alone; countless souls in your reality and in the higher dimensions have gone before you and have lit up the path for you. As you grow, you will help make it easier for others as well. While only you can take the steps to grow, there is much light and assistance available.

One step behind you are hundreds of thousands who are awakening. Remember yourself as you were before you awoke to this path of growth. There are many, many thousands in the world who are at the point of awakening. They may not know yet where to turn or even what information to seek. They are just beginning to question, to listen, and to hear. As you lift the veils and wake up to your path and truth, you will be reaching out to assist them, and they in turn will be reaching out to others.

Humanity is in the process of making an evolutionary leap.

Your energy bodies are evolving; you are gaining a spiritual shimmer and new energies in your aura as you grow spiritually. Because the new human will have a body of light that is able to vibrate at a higher frequency and radiate light, you, your children, and your grandchildren will bring a transformation of consciousness beyond anything you can now imagine.

What you struggle so intently with now—to be more loving, to believe in yourself, to forgive, to have compassion, and to release pain and negativity—will be easier in future times as human energy systems become more evolved. Humanity will have a more fully formed body of light and will become a radiating source of light.

Many of you want this to be your last lifetime on earth, and you speak of "last lifetime" as if it were the ultimate spiritual goal. As you reach higher and higher levels of earth-life mastery, you may or may not choose to return after you die. The earth plane is a beautiful place; you can experience heaven on earth as you become a master of living in higher consciousness. Many highly evolved souls choose to come even though they could live in other dimensions, for they love humanity and the earth itself. Greater levels of mastery also give you an increasing ability to assist others in their growth and an even greater opportunity to grow yourself because of your ability to serve.

You are not on earth because you are too "low" to live in the higher dimensions. Your Higher Self has sent a part of Itself— you—into this dimension to learn more about Its consciousness as expressed in a world of form and matter. Trust that you are here right now because it is the best place for you and offers you the most opportunity to evolve. As you grow and expand, your Higher Self grows and expands. Love your humanity as well as your divinity. What you experience in your daily life— the challenges, feelings, and relationships—are the very things you came to learn from.

The feelings and thoughts you have—all your humanness— offer you a rich and wonderful opportunity to grow and become a source of light to others. As you become more filled with light you assist humanity in reaching "critical mass." When enough people can hold and radiate a larger amount of light, everyone together will take a quantum leap and reach a new evolutionary phase. As more people expand, they will find it easier to be their Higher Selves and reach enlightenment. As more people learn to hold and radiate more light, it will be possible for many others to reach their full potential in this lifetime.

Becoming a Source of Light

MEDITATION

The purpose of this meditation is to lift the veils of unknowing. This will assist you in remembering who you are and gaining a more unlimited view of yourself.

This is a very simple, yet very profound process. You may want a friend to ask you these questions, ask them mentally, or put them on tape and play them back, pausing to give yourself time to answer. If you are alone, you can answer these questions mentally, speak your answers out loud into a tape recorder, or write down your responses.

Steps: Get into your Higher Self state for this meditation.

1. Sit quietly, relax your body, close your eyes, and take a deep breath. Your thoughts are clear and focused, your emotions peaceful and calm. Ask yourself:

   a. Who am I? (If you are asking a friend, ask, "Who are you?")

   b. Where am I from? (If you are asking a friend, ask, "Where are you from?")

   c. Why am I here? (If you are asking a friend, ask, "Why are you here?")

   Each time you ask these questions, put the emphasis on a different word. For instance, you might say, "*Who* am I?" the first time, "Who *am* I?" the second time, and "Who am *I*?" the third. Repeat this sequence several times, and be as imaginative, playful, and creative as you can with your answers.

2. Play as long here as you like. When you are through, return to the room and spend a moment remembering the insights you received. Record them if you like.

16

Enlightenment Through Service

There are many paths to enlightenment. There are paths that involve breathing and posture techniques and others that involve disciplining the will. There are paths that train the mind through meditation. There is a path of devotion and one of willful action. A major opportunity for spiritual growth exists in these times; it is the path of enlightenment through service.

Many of you have come to serve during this time of major transition. Much of your spiritual growth will come through serving and teaching others. You do not need to have a public platform, to be well known, or to do work that others consider important to make an enormous contribution. You can add light to the world through anything you do, through your job, family life, and other activities. Your increasing light will serve others on a telepathic and energy level, for as you grow you will become a transmitter of spiritual energies and make a higher vibration available to everyone around you.

All *teaching is learning.*
All empowerment of others is self-empowerment.

There is no way you can teach and empower others without teaching and empowering yourself. As a teacher, you create the space that allows learning to take place. You empower and teach others every time you create an opportunity for them to grow. By learning to create that space for others to grow spiritually, you grow spiritually yourself. Empowering others will bring you spiritual rewards beyond anything you can imagine.

As you serve others you will gain a radiance and light around you that will create opportunities and good things everywhere you go. You will find increasing prosperity, deep inner satisfaction, and the respect and love of those around you. You will find much energy coming back to you, for every time you create a shift for others you also create a shift to a higher consciousness for yourself. Although you do not want to serve for these reasons, these are some of the gains you may realize as you follow your higher path.

We will call you who are following the path of enlightenment through service "world-servers." Being a world-server means honoring yourself and others; it means thinking of how what you do serves other people. It means coming from your integrity and standing by your deepest values. It means bringing out the best in people, assisting them in discovering their potential and the higher plan of their lives.

Being a world-server means committing to your own growth and following your higher path. It means making a commitment to bringing your life into balance so you can devote a significant portion of your time to your higher purpose. World service comes when you ask for it and are ready. World service comes from doing your life's work and following your higher purpose.

When you first ask for an opportunity to make a difference in the world, you may find yourself putting energy into making your own life work at higher levels. You cannot serve others as effectively if your life is in turmoil and your problems take much of your time and energy. Solving your problems and making your life work is an important part of your spiritual growth.

The more skill you have in manifesting and handling day-to-day issues with clarity and love, the more easily you can accomplish your higher purpose. As your life begins to have more order and harmony you will find many opportunities to make meaningful contributions to others. You will move to a level where much of your growth will come from your world service.

As you reach upward and increase your light, you will draw to yourself all the forms that will make it possible to get your work out to the world. Don't worry if you don't yet know the form of your world service; start with the intention to be of service. Put your life in order. Once you request an opportunity to serve, you are heard by your Higher Self and the higher forces of the universe. Every opportunity will come to you just as soon as you are ready.

Empowering people means
assisting them in making positive changes
in their lives.

Shifting consciousness is an important aspect of your world service. You shift consciousness by empowering people. People make changes when they have new insights and perceptions. They make changes when someone reaches them at the deepest part of their being and touches them with love.

True service comes in moments when there is openness, love, and a lack of boundaries between you and another. It comes when you feel your equality, recognize the other person's divinity, and act in a way that empowers him or her. It comes when you link with a higher power and, through your alignment, allow a greater good to come to both of you. You connect with the other person's Higher Self, and each of you comes away expanded. In those moments you have become the teacher as well as the student.

Empowerment is different from simply helping people. If people are hungry, you can give them food and help them temporarily. They are empowered when you teach them to get food for themselves and they can eat on an ongoing basis. If you are a healer, you can keep "fixing" people's problems, or you can teach them how to solve their own problems. Empowerment means teaching people skills they can use to take charge of their own lives rather than bailing them out of recurring problems. Empowerment means loving people rather than saving them. Ask yourself, "How does what I am doing serve this person to become more self-sufficient and independent?"

When you assist people, perhaps helping them find solutions to problems, they either remain the same or make positive changes in their lives. If they make changes, you have shifted their consciousness and made a true contribution to them. Then they will have more choices and higher visions of themselves, which they can use to create better lives.

To shift consciousness you need to recognize where you can truly make a difference. It requires knowing when people are open to growing and giving them assistance only if they are ready. This way, you will gain much energy from your contact, and your time with this person will contribute to your spiritual growth.

You do not want to go on a crusade and convince others that they must change before they are ready. A crusade to reform people or society simply causes separation and wastes a lot of your valuable energy. Instead, you can help people shift their consciousness and make a lasting contribution to their lives.

You may wonder how you can help with the pressing social

and environmental issues of these times. One of the most important things you can do is to help people shift to a higher consciousness. At a higher level, they will take more responsibility for themselves, for their society, and for the environment. When a higher consciousness exists in enough people, solutions to these pressing issues will be found.

Consciousness can be shifted in simple ways. When you are with children or friends, focus on what you can do that will create a shift for them. When you meet people, think of what you can contribute to them, not what you will get from them. If you are getting together with friends, ask what you could do together that will expand each of you. Ask yourself, "How can I serve them with my words or actions?" Any time you come from your heart, speak with love, and assist people in recognizing their divinity you shift their consciousness.

Even when you meet with a business client, ask, "What is the higher purpose of this call or visit? How can I make a contribution to this person's life? How can my work, product, advice, or service empower this person?" As you do this regularly, you will lift your friendships to a higher level and evolve more rapidly yourself. You may find many wonderful surprises and much business success as you start focusing on serving other people.

One woman invented games to empower her friends when they were together. She would have them all pretend it was one year in the future and talk about all the good things they had accomplished in the past year. She took every opportunity to draw people's higher vision out of them, helping them express it in words and encouraging them to create it. Her company was much sought after.

You can shift consciousness in small children by contacting their Higher Selves, even for a moment. Imagine your Higher Self contacting Theirs, telling them mentally, "I see the beauty and light in you; I recognize you for the great being you are." Children will usually respond in some way to your silent message, and you will have assisted in their spiritual awakening.

You can help lift the vibratory note of everyone by imagining that everything you do to empower others goes out to everyone else who needs this assistance. For instance, as you assist one person, imagine that you are assisting everyone with the same problem. As you help and love your own child, imagine that your love is going out to every child who could use that love right now.

> # It *is important to know*
> *when to assist people*
> *and when not to.*

It takes a certain amount of your energy to shift someone's consciousness to a higher level. It is important to learn how much energy to put out to create that shift. You may have experienced helping someone with just a few words of advice. He or she made changes and solved the problem. You probably felt good and energized by the exchange.

You may have had other exchanges with friends in which you poured a lot of energy into assisting them, but their recurring problems never got solved. You probably felt drained, for the energy you put out didn't create any lasting changes in their lives. If you choose the wrong time to help or if the person isn't open to growing, you will put out much energy with little result. You also need to learn how much energy you are capable of shifting so that you do not take on more than you can handle.

Are there people you are sending a lot of energy to who aren't growing, or who feel like burdens to you in some way? In your mind, imagine you are putting these burdens down. Turn these people over to their own Higher Selves to help them grow. Send them light, and release your responsibility for making their lives work. Some of you will know you are carrying people because you have shoulder and back problems.

Often your back hurts because you are carrying too much responsibility and too many burdens that are not yours.

The higher your consciousness, the more of a penalty you pay for putting your energy where it doesn't create a shift. You may feel tired or drained, or even get sick. When you create a shift, you feel charged with energy and your radiance increases. As you grow, you will want to be increasingly alert to whom and what you are putting your time and energy into and the results you are or aren't creating.

If people feel like burdens, it is a sign that "carrying" them is not for their higher good. You may be taking away their lessons and slowing down their growth. They may become dependent on you and stop taking responsibility for making their own lives work. People who are growing rapidly from your assistance will not feel like burdens.

One woman's close friend was constantly in turmoil; she had a series of unhappy relationships and was unable to find a job she liked. For months the woman spent hours counseling her friend and even helped her search for a good job. Yet nothing seemed to change; the relationships continued to be in turmoil and no job was good enough for her friend. The woman felt increasingly drained and began to realize she was carrying her friend's burdens as if they were her own. Her friend wasn't using her guidance to grow. She mentally took the burdens off her shoulders and sent her friend light. She let her know gently that she was no longer interested in trying to solve her friend's problems for her, and she also let her friend know she loved her just as she was. Shortly thereafter, the woman met a new friend who was a joy to be with. The old friend simply found another person she could complain to, and her life didn't improve.

In our realms, serving others is a great honor and requires much study, self-observation, and spiritual attainment. One's mastery is demonstrated by how much of a shift is created with each energy expenditure. The higher your consciousness, the more energy you can shift with the same output of your own energy. As you achieve mastery, you learn to expend a small amount of energy in the right place at the right time and create an enormous shift that assists many people.

I have given this to Sanaya as my main criterion for our work together: whatever we do must make a lasting and significant contribution to other people. The way I can serve you best is to give you a direct experience of your own power. This can be done through teaching you higher states of consciousness and other skills that allow you to get your own answers. This can be done also by simply loving you and reflecting back to you your beauty, wisdom, and compassion.

Before I undertake any project or work with anyone, I question, "How much opportunity is there for me to make a lasting contribution to this person or these people?" I look over all the possible areas I could put my energy and then choose those that can make the greatest shift for people.

You can talk directly to people's Higher Selves.

Get quiet and mentally ask people's Higher Selves if it is appropriate for you to give assistance, or if they still need to learn the lessons their problems are teaching them. You will get a definite sense of whether or not it is all right to assist them. If you get no answer, wait before you assist them, and ask again at another time. Don't take action until you get a sense that it is appropriate to help them in the way you are thinking about.

You can also ask your own Higher Self for a symbol, picture, or message about how ready people are to grow and how much assistance to give them. If they are ready for your assistance, ask what you could do that would create the most shift for them. Sometimes people are not ready to grow or change. Simply love them, acknowledge their divinity, and allow them to be just as they are.

One woman was putting out a tremendous amount of energy to help a depressed friend and felt exhausted when he didn't respond to her encouragement. She asked for a symbol of his condition, and inwardly saw him as very compressed dry ground with a few drops of water on top. The water couldn't seep into the soil because the ground was too dry and compacted. She realized that she—the water—couldn't get through to him, and that she was wasting her energy by trying to help. She sent him light and a mental message that she loved him and stopped pouring out her energy.

When you tune in to people before you assist them and get a feeling of "No, don't give assistance now," simply send them light to use as they want, and let go of any discomfort you may have about watching them learn their lessons. Sometimes you won't get a message; you will just have a feeling of resistance about helping them. Recognize that people aren't always ready to let go of their current crises or problems and there are times when you can't create a shift, no matter how much energy you pour into other people. Their Higher Selves have put them in these situations to help them grow, and they may still be learning lessons from being in these situations. When people are ready to make a shift, you will rarely have any resistance to assisting them.

To serve others, you will need compassion and the ability to detach. Compassion is helping people understand what they are learning and empowering them to see the gifts in what they are experiencing. It is watching others go through their lessons the way they have chosen to experience them, knowing that though they may be suffering at the personality level, their suffering will help them give birth to a new, stronger self. Assist them by focusing on all the gifts their problems are offering them, such as teaching them about self-love, compassion, patience, inner strength, and other positive qualities.

Assist people at whatever level they understand. Before people are aware that they create their own realities, their truth may be that they are victims of fate or circumstance. At this level, telling them that they created the circumstances they are experiencing will only make them feel guilty and set them back. If someone you know is sick and not yet at the level to understand he has created his illness to grow, telling him he created his sickness may only make him feel worse. Assist people on the levels they are at, and only when they are ready help them see how they created their problems.

One person CAN make an enormous difference.

Becoming a world-server means joining the higher community of beings working together to bring light and evolution to others. Your own growth will accelerate rapidly, and you will become magnetic to people and opportunities that allow you to make a difference. Your world service is in whatever area you are drawn to—peace, ecology, education, the arts, medicine, science, metaphysics, or others. You can be of service in any job you have. You are in exactly the right place now to start serving and empowering others.

To awaken others, be on fire yourself, aglow with your own inner light. One of the greatest gifts you give the world is to feel enthusiastic and charged with energy, loving your work and your life. Draw other people to you with your enthusiasm. Radiate those qualities you want to see in others.

As you grow, things will become very easy for you to accomplish; it is important not to brag about your successes. Rather than focusing on your accomplishments, acknowledge the accomplishments of your friends. Applaud people whenever they shift or take a step.

It takes only a few people living at a higher vibration to create a doorway for many others. Becoming a world-server is one of the fastest paths to enlightenment and will bring you joy, abundance, and inner satisfaction. Make the most of every opportunity you have to serve and empower others. As you do, you will reach enlightenment through service.

Enlightenment Through Service

MEDITATION

The purpose of this meditation is to ask for your world service to increase.

Steps: You might want to have a crystal nearby that you can hold in your hand.

1. Call light to you and imagine you are in a cocoon of light that carries you to a temple where many high beings are gathered. As you approach this temple, feel the beautiful energy of peace, love, and joy that is present. You are greeted by your Higher Self, who leads you to sit or stand in the center of a circle of many high beings. You will be participating in a ceremony to celebrate your commitment to greater world service.

2. Your Higher Self and these high beings are holding open a symbolic doorway for you, a doorway to your higher path and world service. On the other side of this doorway is much light and accelerated spiritual growth. Walking through this doorway will make very real changes in your life. You will attract more opportunities to make a meaningful contribution. Walking through this doorway is making a very real commitment to your greater world service; take all the time you need to think about it. When you are ready, walk through the doorway.

3. After you go through this doorway, many high beings come over, one at a time, to give you special gifts to help you with your world service. Imagine some of these beings

and the gifts they are giving you. Realize all the love and support you have as you carry out your higher purpose.

4. Pick up your crystal and hold it in your hand near your heart. Ask for more world service, and affirm that you are ready for it. Ask to have more revealed to you about the nature of your higher purpose and path of world service. Your Higher Self and these beings will energize your crystal and send you energy for your world service. In the future, you can hold your crystal and it will help you energize your world service.

5. Your Higher Self comes over to you, and you begin to merge and become one. You are now one with your Higher Self. The high beings present invite you to join them in sending out a wake-up call, inviting all who are ready to wake up to their Higher Selves. To do so, charge yourself with light and then allow light to flow out of you, joining with the light of all beings present. This light is sent to all who are awakening to their inner light. You are becoming a source of light and awakening to others. Feel energy pouring through you.

6. If you would like to send a telepathic message to the Higher Self of someone, do so now. Make the message as loving and as high as you can. Let your Higher Self make your energy even more beautiful, then send energy from your heart to this person's.

7. Stay as long as it feels comfortable. When you are ready, mentally thank and bid good-bye to these beings. Return to the room and feel your increased light and inner peace.

As you send light you increase your own radiance and spiritual growth. As you become a greater source of light, you will constantly be sent light, energy, and love to assist you with your work.

17

Lifting the Veils of Illusion

Lifting the veils of illusion means being able to remember who you are and what your higher purpose is. It is going beyond the illusions created by living in the density of matter and remembering the truth of the higher realms. It is knowing that your consciousness is your primary, causal reality. It is learning to see the world through the eyes of your Higher Self, knowing what is truth and what is illusion.

Reality and truth depend upon your rate of vibration. The higher your vibration the more you are able to love yourself and view others with compassion. At one level of vibration, revenge may be a way to handle the feeling of being wronged; revenge would be that person's truth. At a higher vibration a person might understand cause and effect and know the power of sending love to one who wronged him or her. As you increase your rate of vibration, your truth will expand and the veils of illusion will disappear.

Illusions promise to give you one thing but actually give you something else. You may have experienced this when you got something you wanted and it didn't give you what you thought it would. One woman thought all her problems with her husband would be solved by having a baby. After having one, she realized that the baby brought her much joy but didn't solve the problems she had with her husband. Some people think that material wealth will solve all their problems. They often learn as they accumulate money that their problems increase unless they work directly on solving them. They come to realize that money cannot give them inner peace, solve their relationship problems, or make them feel safe until they work directly on those issues.

How might your life change if all the illusions were gone and you could know a higher truth? You would create those things that fulfilled you and best represented who you are. You would be able to accurately assess situations and know what action to take to produce the results you wanted. You would know what level to come from as you talked and worked with people, because you would recognize the level of their understanding and development. You would tell yourself the truth about how things are and look beyond appearances to know what is real. You would not necessarily believe in what you were told; you would know what was true for you. You would stand by your beliefs, even if others around you believed in something different.

You would have a clear vision of your purpose and know what actions to take to accomplish it. You would see beyond people's personalities to their Higher Selves. You would not let self-doubts or thoughts that you weren't good enough pull you from your path. Believing in yourself and your path, you would have greater strength and courage to carry out your work.

When you were very young, some of you did not want to see your reality as it was and slowly closed down your vision. Some of you literally reduced your "seeing" and had to wear glasses to restore your vision. Affirm that you are now ready to see the world clearly. Some people find their eyesight improving when they decide they are willing to see the world as it really is and lift the veils of illusion.

Let go of your judgments
to see beyond illusions.

Judgments stop you from seeing things as they really are. Learn to observe without comparing, projecting your thoughts onto others, evaluating, or making up stories about what is happening.

For instance, you watch a sunset. You might say, "The warm and loving sun gently laid herself to rest behind the tired old hills, sighing as she spread the last of her glory over the land." Or, you could say, "The sun went down behind the hills and there were strands of gold and red in the sky." The latter way describes things just as they are without adding your interpretations or feelings. How much do you color what you perceive with your judgments, projections, or interpretations? Practice describing things to yourself just as they are without any stories describing them and you will see beyond the illusions created by your perceptions.

To understand how you project your feelings about things onto other people, take any object and place it in front of you. Mentally describe to yourself how it feels. You may realize how much of your world view and feelings you project onto others as you do this. For instance, one girl, looking at a chair, said that the chair felt tired of having people sitting on it all day, never appreciating the load it was carrying. She projected onto the chair her feelings that people "used" her and didn't appreciate the load she was carrying.

When you judge others, you are often projecting your thoughts about reality onto them. Those thoughts may not describe them accurately at all! For instance, if you see people yelling at their children in a store, you might think they are bad parents. Instead, they may be tired, under pressure, or doing just what is perfect for their children at that moment. Sending them love will do more to lift them than your negative judgments. As you get beyond judgment and learn to see people through the eyes of compassion, you will feel an increasing oneness with them.

Watch people without making any judgments about who they are, and you will sense more about them. Find something beautiful about each person and practice sending light or love to him or her through your eyes and heart. You cannot serve people when you separate yourself from them by judging them. We guides and your Higher Self do not judge you; we send you a steady stream of love and focus on how good and beautiful you are. By focusing on what is good in you, we empower you to be all you can be.

You may have illusions about who people are because of your attachments to them. Because many of you are natural healers and teachers, you have the ability to perceive how people might fulfill more of their potential. Some of you are living for the day when your loved ones will become all you know they can be. You may not want to face the reality of who they are right now. Although it is good to hold a high vision of people, it is also important to see them clearly and love them for who they are right now.

Do you live with a fantasy of who someone might become and not accept this person as he or she is? Or do you see your loved ones without illusions and love them just as they are? You can assist them in growing by focusing on their strengths rather than their weaknesses. Acknowledge their divinity.

Illusions can come when you look only at the surface of something and don't go beyond appearances to examine what is inside. This is like buying a house based on its outside appearance, without examining the interior. You sometimes do this with people when you judge them by their appearances without getting to know them. Great masters have no trouble walking unrecognized among you. All they do is assume the appearance of someone who doesn't meet your picture of what a high being ought to look like—and you never recognize them.

Learn to see the bigger picture of who people are by looking beyond the roles they play. As you do, you are going beyond outer appearances and seeing the reality of their Higher Selves. Relate what they are doing with their lives to its higher purpose for them. For instance, someone whose job is typing may be using that activity to learn how to connect her mind with her hands. It may be a necessary step for her to open to her higher path of healing through her hands. Carpenters may be learning to bring their and others' visions from the abstract mental planes into physical reality. Think of a friend and his or her job. See if you can find a deeper meaning for this job. You cannot tell who people are from their earthly activities.

It is an illusion to think that if you are spiritually evolved you must be famous or highly visible as a spiritual leader. Many high beings live alone, working telepathically on the inner planes of reality to broadcast peace and answer the calls for guidance from awakening souls. Many have quiet positions of service as gardeners, teachers of children, potters, and caretakers. Only a few high beings volunteer to be visible. Fame and wealth do not indicate one's enlightenment; both highly evolved and less evolved people have fame and wealth.

*Illusions come from accepting
others' thoughts and beliefs
without questioning their value to you.*

Mass agreement that things are a certain way can create illusions. Whole populations can believe something to be true until someone proves differently. At one time it was thought that the sun revolved around the earth. A few individuals have changed the course of history by questioning such mass beliefs and having the courage to explore their new theories.

You are the healers, teachers, and leaders; you came to create new possibilities and bring through higher truths about abundance, planetary peace, ecology, and more. To do that you need to see the world clearly. Don't accept things just because others do. Question what you are hearing and reading. Learn to go beyond what is commonly held to be true and discover your own truth. Through your ideas about food, healing with energy, ecology, peace, animal rights, human rights, and other issues you are bringing a higher truth to the earth plane. Follow your heart and believe in your truth, not what others or society tells you is best. As you discover what is true for you, you will assist others in finding a higher way by your example.

How do you lift the veils of illusion? You start by asking your Higher Self to lift them and being willing to see what is revealed. Question things you have taken for granted. Explore new areas. Imagine you are a small child or that you have just arrived on the planet and are examining things for the first time.

Integrity is living the truth you know.

Integrity is an important aspect of spiritual growth. It is acting, talking, and behaving in ways that honor yourself and others. It is examining things before you do them and doing only those things you know to be true. Living in integrity—in harmony with your beliefs and values—will accelerate your growth and make the process more joyful. Integrity will bring clarity and order to every area of your life. Examine the opportunities that come your way and choose to take them not because they seem glamorous but because they make a contribution to others.

To lift the veils of illusion you will need to learn your truth and come from your integrity. You may be challenged to come from your heart with people rather than from your will. To follow your heart is to find a higher truth. You can find a higher truth by focusing on serving others. Put yourself in the other person's shoes, and do only those things that honor both of you. Know what your deeper values are and follow them. Find a way for both of you to win, rather than thinking that one of you must lose if the other is to win.

Coming from your integrity and seeing through illusions takes courage. Before you lift the veils of illusion you may not be certain you will like what you see. Once you lift them, you will gain a greater ability to know truth and recognize your and others' Higher Selves. You will be able to focus on your higher purpose and become your own authority. As you lift the veils of illusion, you will gain enormous rewards; true spiritual power comes from being able to see things clearly.

Lifting the Veils of Illusion

MEDITATION

The purpose of this meditation is to lift the veils of illusion and see what is real. You will know your truth, what is on your path, and what isn't.

Steps:

1. Take a deep breath, relax your body, and call light to yourself. In your cocoon of light, travel to the temple where many high beings are present. Your Higher Self meets you as you arrive, leading you to a beautiful courtyard where you are joined by many other high beings. Your Higher Self is standing by your side.

2. Your Higher Self asks you if you are truly ready to lift the veils of illusion. Go within and decide whether you are ready to see reality clearly and to look at other people and know them without illusions. Are you ready to be your own authority and trust your own wisdom? Your world is going to look different without these veils.

3. Once you decide you are ready, all beings present are going to assist you by sending you light as your Higher Self starts lifting the veils. Say, "I am ready to KNOW. I am ready to SEE. I am ready to BE truth." As you say these words, imagine all the beings present are sending you light and energy to lift these veils. Take a deep breath, and feel the veils being lifted.

4. After you lift the veils, begin to merge with your Higher Self. Feel your Higher Self merging with you even more completely, now that you are willing to know, see, and be truth. You and your Higher Self are now one.

5. Feel the joy and celebration as you lift the veils. You are now able to see reality through the eyes of your Higher Self in every area of your life. Sit in this light for a while and imagine the sun beaming down on you, dissolving all the fog that has kept you from seeing reality clearly. Feel how open, expanded, and clear you are becoming.

6. This is very real; you *will* begin to see things differently. It will happen at a pace that is comfortable to you and aligned with your growth. Bask in the light and love that is present around you, and return to the room when you are ready.

18

Communicating as Your Higher Self

As you grow and evolve, the words you speak and the thoughts you have about others will have an increasing power to affect people. Your positive thoughts and visions of people will lift them higher. Your criticism will depress their energies and hold them back. To go higher it is important that you learn the power of the words you speak. In the higher realms, every sound, thought, and spoken word produces strong effects, so it is important to learn to communicate in loving ways.

There are many ways to communicate, including telepathically, in which messages are sent and received mentally; body language, which is communicating through positions, movements, and gestures; and verbal communication. You can learn to communicate as your Higher Self. Higher Self communication brings energy and love back to you. It gives energy and love to others. When you speak as your Higher Self the people around you will be open and responsive to what you have to say. You will speak the truth with precision and create peace and harmony.

All *Higher Self communication begins in the heart.*

It is important to come from your heart when you speak. When you speak with love, truly caring for the higher good of other people, you create a real connection. When your words are chosen with care and spoken with the intent to serve, they empower people to grow. When you have the intention to serve another person's higher good with what you say, your words have an increasing ability to shift that person's consciousness. Before you meet with people or speak to them for the first time, imagine talking from your heart to theirs. Ask for the highest good to come from your time together.

Sound is a very powerful way of creating higher consciousness, whether it is made by your voice or musical instruments. Many of you have come to earth at this time to use sound to raise consciousness. You may find yourself in positions where you speak to others, play or create music, channel, and so on.

All communication begins with a telepathic connection, whether or not you are aware of it. Before you talk, you are aware at some level of the other person. You can increase this awareness and notice as you talk whether the other person is listening, interested, or agreeing with you. Note what level of understanding he or she has about what you are saying. Use terms the other person can understand. It is important to talk at the level of your audience; you would talk to a five-year-old in a different way than you would talk to a ten-year-old. If you stop for a moment before you speak and sense who your listeners are, you will be able to talk with much greater effectiveness.

Because all communication starts on the nonverbal, telepathic level, you can send messages to someone telepathically and create changes in your relationship without saying a word. If you want to talk about a difficult issue with a loved one, spend time working on the issue by telepathically sending love before you speak. Wait to speak until you feel a heart connection and the other person's readiness to hear what you have to say.

As you learn to communicate as your Higher Self, you may find yourself talking less often. There is great power in silence. You will discover increasing joy and deep harmony with your loved ones when you link with them silently.

The next time you are with someone you love, explore what a silent connection is like. During your time together, ask them to create ten minutes of quiet with you. You may discover an even richer connection than when you talk, for you will be joining as your Higher Selves. You often experience this when you are apart from each other, for when you get back together after a physical separation, you often feel even more loving and connected. In the silence you have developed a stronger bond through your telepathic connection.

Your words create what you speak about.
Learn to speak positively.

When you speak, be as harmonious and loving as possible. You might imagine that you are sending out waves of harmony and peace to others as you talk. Be alert to how people are responding to what you are saying. If they resist you, if you aren't in a supportive environment, don't talk or try to convince others. A lot of your energy is sent out through your words; talk only when your words can make a contribution to others and they are listening. Then you will get more energy back than you send out.

Speaking positive, uplifting words creates a higher reality for you and others, for every word you speak powerfully creates what you talk about. For instance, when you walk in the door and greet your mate, many of you immediately list all the frustrating things that happened during the day. Instead, talk about things that have meaning to you. Talk about a new insight or discovery you made during the day. Share a positive experience that happened while you were away. Talking about positive, meaningful things lifts your and other people's energies higher and establishes a deeper connection.

Some of you are afraid to speak of what you believe in, especially things that aren't accepted by the masses. You may have faint past-life memories of being persecuted for speaking your truth. Some of you believe that others won't love you if you speak the truth, and you repress the things you need to say to your loved ones. You may be afraid to speak up and go along for a while doing things you don't really want to do. If you do, your pent-up energy eventually will come out as a burst of anger or tears.

You don't need to repress your thoughts and feelings; you can voice your thoughts as they come up in a way that is loving and serves the other person. It is much better to give people a chance to love you as you are than to act in ways you think will make them love you. You can only pretend for so long to be who you aren't; it is a greater gift to give someone the opportunity to love you just as you are from the beginning. Tell yourself, "I am lovable. I will be loved even when I express my wants and needs."

When you first begin expressing your feelings, you may not always do so in a way that is as loving as you would want. Love yourself for having the courage to speak up, and affirm that next time you will be even more loving and speak more as your Higher Self. People who are used to getting their way may not be happy at first when you begin to speak up. Let them have their surprise or upset and continue to speak truthfully. Speak with the intent to serve the other person; assign no blame, speak lovingly, and take responsibility for how you feel.

*As you grow spiritually
your words gain more power to affect people.*

You have the ability to lift people's energies with your encouragement and the ability to dampen people's energies by criticizing them. If you find something in people to criticize, realize that this is the very area you could empower them in. If you catch yourself criticizing people, take the area you are criticizing them for and imagine them growing and evolving in that area.

As you grow spiritually, people will call on you to guide them in their growth. Your ability to give feedback is an important skill. Good feedback, given in the right way, can make an enormous difference in people's ability to grow. Good feedback always empowers people. It points them in the direction of their next step and makes it easier for them to take it.

When you need to give feedback to people, do you tell them the truth if you think that doing so might hurt their feelings? To give feedback to others, start by getting peaceful and centered. Think of what you want to tell them. Ask your Higher Self if correcting them or giving them advice will truly serve them. Are they ready to hear your advice, or will it simply close down the energy between you? Sometimes it is best not to speak of your observations; not every thought has to be verbally expressed. Some people are not ready to hear what you have to say.

It is better to say only those things that serve people in some way. All things can be said in a way that is empowering and loving. Truly loving energy will always be felt. When your intent is to love and serve others and what you say comes from your heart, you will assist people in growing. There is always a higher truth, a way to say things that leaves other people feeling good about who they are. If you need to correct people's behaviors and give them feedback about how they can do better, learn to do it in a way that serves them and with the intent to make them feel good about who they are.

This does not mean their personalities are always going to like what you say. Sometimes the truth you communicate to others may not be comfortable to them at the personality level.

If your communication comes from the heart and is given with the intent to serve, it is a gift that will contribute to others' growth.

Before you speak, ask yourself how what you plan to say will contribute to people's lives.

Ask yourself, "How does what I am telling people contribute to their growth?" If all you want to do is vent your angry feelings, do not speak to them. Write a letter and don't mail it, or talk out loud to yourself until you are ready to speak in a responsible, loving way.

Higher communication does not blame or make the other person wrong; it creates an opening for that person to grow. Telling the truth with love will serve others when you take responsibility for your feelings and blame no one for the way you feel. Say what you feel or think with tact and kindness, and you will gain more in the long run than if you speak with anger.

If you start your communication with praise and recognition of the other person, you will have more of his or her attention. You may have noticed that when someone congratulated or praised you, you felt good and listened to that person. Acknowledge people and you will have a more attentive audience.

What if people you love won't talk to you at the deep and meaningful levels you want them to? Start by communicating with them telepathically. Send them a mental message that you love and accept them exactly as they are. Make a decision that you will speak to them only when you can say something loving and supportive. You will notice that they listen more often, and opportunities will arise for you to connect in more meaningful ways.

One woman was disappointed by her husband's not showing affection. Rather than telling him directly that she wanted more signs of affection, she would sulk or act distant. He didn't get her messages, and she grew more frustrated. She didn't feel it was all right to simply ask for what she wanted. One day she decided to tell him directly how she felt, without blaming or making him wrong.

She started by telling him of the things she liked about him and their relationship. He listened. She told him an occasional hug meant a lot to her and she missed physical expressions of affection. He hadn't realized this and explained that in his family people only expressed affection openly when someone was unable to cope. To him, giving physical affection was a message to the other person that he or she was weak. With their talk, she became more understanding of his resistance to affection, and he became more aware of her need for it. They were then able to work together to find mutually acceptable solutions.

If you focus on people's behaviors that you do not like, you may elicit more of the same behaviors from them. One way to make it easier for people to respond in higher ways is to praise a part of their behavior you like. Try this with a loved one. Every time this person does something you like, praise him or her. Ignore behaviors you don't like.

One man did this with his wife and was amazed at the results. Before he changed his approach, he was constantly after her to lose some weight she had gained, and frequently made fun of her eating habits. Afterward, he acknowledged every time she looked good or ate healthy foods. He started treating her as if they were dating again, making her feel loved and special. When he stopped making her wrong for gaining weight, she responded by slowly changing her eating habits, and she even lost weight. Criticizing people almost always alienates them and makes it harder for them to change their behavior. Most people will respond more to praise than to criticism.

How would you respond if your partner or spouse came to you and told you all the things about you he or she liked? You would probably do those things more often. You would be more likely to listen to other things this person told you as well. When you focus on the good in people, you empower them to create more of the behavior that expresses their goodness.

If you want smooth, clear communication, before you start speaking make sure it is a good time and the other person is really listening. To truly communicate you need to make contact. Speak only when there is a connection, or else you will send out energy with no real purpose and you may feel drained. Think of several specific points you want to make, for it is better to focus clearly on a few issues than to cover too many.

All communication starts with a picture or feeling of something you want to communicate. For fun, ask several friends to describe the picture that appears in their minds as you ask them to think of a beautiful meadow. Each person will make a picture that is unique to him or her, and those pictures may be very different from yours. That is why you can think you said one thing but the other person might think you said something else. Present your thoughts as clearly as possible and pay attention to the other person's response to make sure he or she understands your meaning.

You can have what you want. Express yourself with precision.

People filter what they hear through their belief systems. They will color your messages with their thoughts and emotions. You might say to your mate, "I would like you to do the dishes tonight." Your mate may hear you imply, "You never do anything; I wish you would help out now and then," or even, "I'm really unhappy with our relationship." The message can take on a different meaning for them, even though all you are thinking about is how tired you are. Often what you say and what other people hear you say are two very different things.

Say what you want. People usually prefer definite guidelines to vague, undefined expectations. For instance, you may have your children or a housekeeper helping you clean your house. If cleaning includes many small details that are important to you, ask for exactly what you want. Many of you expect others to have the same picture of a "clean house" as you do. To some people a clean kitchen means the dishes are put away and the kitchen counter is clean. To others it means the appliances are polished, the cupboard doors are clean, and the floor is waxed. If you aren't precise, you may be disappointed in the poor job they do by your standards, when in fact they are doing an excellent job by theirs.

You can communicate as your Higher Self. Stop for a moment before you speak and ask yourself, "How would I speak as my Higher Self? What would I say, and how would I say it?" As you do this, you are bringing the energy of your Higher Self into your throat center of communication. Explore what your Higher Self might say. Bringing your Higher Self into all your communications will greatly increase the harmony, peace, and love in your life. As you do you can make a true contribution to others as you empower them with your words and thoughts.

Communicating as Your Higher Self

MEDITATION

The purpose of this meditation is to open your throat center and link it with your Higher Self.

Steps: Get into your Higher Self state for this meditation.

1. Put your attention on the area of your throat, and let the high, fine vibration of your Higher Self come into every cell and atom in this area. As your Higher Self, you are opening and adding light to your throat area. Then, send love from your heart into your throat area, so that everything you say comes from your heart.

2. Begin to speak as your Higher Self. You might want to start with an "Om" or an extended "Ahhh." Notice if the voice of your Higher Self is slower, lower, more resonant, or richer than your normal voice.

3. As your Higher Self, give yourself a message about how you can communicate in a higher way and how you can open your throat center. Speak the answers out loud, noticing the tonal qualities of your Higher Self voice.

4. You may want to finish with a series of Oms. Play with them and make them as beautiful and melodic as you can. Feel the energy of the Oms as they affect your entire body. The sound of Om can assist you in opening your spiritual center and linking your throat with your Higher Self. Find an opportunity today or tomorrow to speak as your Higher Self when you are talking to someone.

19

Right Use of Will

As the energy vibrations you live in move up to a new, higher octave, one of your energy centers is changing dramatically. This is the "center of will" located at your solar plexus. Humanity is moving away from having its consciousness focused in the center of will, toward having its consciousness focused in the heart center of love.

You live on a planet of free will, and your will is one of the most magnificent and powerful parts of your being. It puts into form and action the spiritual energies you are receiving from the Higher Will. Your will carries out your choices and decisions, seeks truth, and helps you stand up for what you believe in. Your will sees to it that you are self-determining and self-directing. One of the most wonderful, challenging aspects of earth-reality is learning to use your will to manifest your higher good and flow in harmony with the Higher Will.

Using your will can be compared to driving a car. Like a car, your will is the vehicle you use to get places. Your will can put on the brakes and slow things down or press the gas pedal and speed things up. Like a steering wheel, your will can steer you in many directions. When you align your will with your personality, it is like having a reliable car that is easy to drive. You get to where you want to go easily. If you don't know how to use your will, it can be like a car you can't count on; you may not get to where you want to go.

In the past, a strong will was needed. Force and aggression assured survival against harsh elements. Today, an aggressive, dominant will is no longer necessary for survival. In these times it is important to use your will in softer, more skillful ways, relying not on force but on love and creativity to get things done.

Trust that the universe is working FOR you and WITH you.

Many cultures teach you that to get what you want you must push very hard, be manipulative or aggressive, and battle your way through obstacles. This view is based on an underlying assumption that the universe is against you and must be conquered. If you use your will as if there is an opposing force, you actually create opposing forces where there are none. Start by assuming the universe is working for you and with you to assist you in creating your higher good.

Many of you were independent, stubborn, and even rebellious as children. You needed a strong will, because you knew you would be bringing new thoughts and ideas to the world. You needed to believe in yourself even when people around you didn't support your ideas. You can now use the strength of your will to develop a wise and magnetic will and have things come to you more easily.

Don't make yourself wrong if you had to use a lot of force and will to get things done in the past, for you were doing the best you knew how. You were developing a strong will of your own by creating obstacles and opposing forces to push against. It is important to have a well-developed will, for you are a creative partner with the higher forces of the universe; your will is necessary to carry out your part in the work of transformation.

Your *will is much wiser than you think.*

As you grow spiritually you will learn to use your magnetic and wise will rather than your forceful will. A wise will is one that does things with thought, planning, and intention. It thinks of better ways than force to do things. For instance, one mother tried using force to get her children to go to bed on time and stay put. She would yell, plead, and threaten. Using her wise will, she devised a technique that worked and didn't involve force. She gave her children a choice of going to bed early and having her read them a story or staying up half an hour later and not having a story. Having a choice, they usually chose the story, and fell asleep peacefully afterward. There was no longer a battle of wills. She solved the problem by being wise and loving rather than forceful.

Your wise will surveys all the circumstances surrounding the issues and finds effective ways to do things with a minimum of effort. It waits until the time is right to make a move, knowing that if the time isn't right, things will take a lot more energy to accomplish. Your wise will is patient, knowing that some things take time to accomplish. It persistently and consistently contributes the energy needed to create your goals, knowing that you don't have to do things all at once. It takes the time and steps it needs to do a good job.

Your wise will is confident, tries out new solutions, and takes the initiative. It looks for new, better ways to do things. It makes decisions not solely based on impulsive feelings but by blending them with logic and common sense.

When the actions you take are aligned with your Higher Self, you will not need force to carry them out. When you are working toward your higher goals you may need to work steadily and persistently, but you will not be pushing against resistant, unmoving forces.

You can use your forceful will on yourself, forcing yourself to do things, but not for long. Your intellect often sets goals for you and wants your forceful will to carry them out. Your forceful will may try to do what your intellect tells it to, but if your goal or the way you are pursuing it isn't for your higher good, your wise will will stop you. Your wise will follows the guidance of your Higher Self.

Your wise will is connected to the Higher Will and your Higher Self. Your wise will won't let itself be used against you; it is too powerful a force for your intellect to control. Be grateful that this powerful part of your will does not let you do things for long that aren't for your higher good. You may succeed for a while in forcing yourself to do things, but not for long.

Your intellect may decide that you need to lose 10 pounds, completely change your eating habits, and redo your life over-night, but that doesn't mean those changes are for your higher good. If you use your forceful will to diet, you may succeed for a while, then go back to your old eating habits and gain the weight back.

When your Higher Self feels it is better for you not to do something, It goes to your wise will and says, "Create resistance; stop; do not carry through with the action." When it is good for you to do something you will feel a desire to do it; you will be drawn to it because it is something you love and not something you are forcing yourself to do.

You only stick to those things you love; your forceful will only succeeds temporarily in getting you to do things your Higher Self isn't guiding you to do. For instance, if you enjoy being slimmer and eating the healthier foods you eat while dieting, gradually you will be drawn to eat healthier and be slimmer because you value and love those things. Then it is not your forceful will but your wise will that is guiding you. When you do what you love, it requires no force. The only things you do without resistance are those things you love to do and are drawn to. Through trial and error your experiences teach you what these things are.

The more you use your forceful will to make yourself do something, the more you can push yourself into an opposite reaction. One man who jogged three times a week decided to increase his running to six times a week and to take up bicycling and swimming at the same time. He had decided intellectually he needed to be more of an athlete. He forced himself to continue this program for a month, although he became sore and exhausted. He finally quit not only the new exercise program but his original running program as well. It took him months to start exercising again.

You may say, "I know I really need to lose weight, get fit, do this project, let go of this person, and so on. Why isn't my will cooperating?" Your wise will has your higher interests in mind. Even though a part of you thinks it might be best to do something, if another part of you is resisting, trust that there is a higher reason why you are avoiding this. If you aren't accomplishing a goal your intellect has set, rather than forcing yourself to do it, talk to your wise will. Ask, "Why won't you do what I am telling you to do?" Perhaps whatever you are planning is too drastic a measure to take that would not be in harmony with the rest of your life and path. Keep your goal in mind and ask your wise will what plan of action it WILL work with you to accomplish.

Your wise will guides you to those things you love to do. Before you decide to do something, get quiet and notice your feelings about doing it. Ask yourself before you take action, "Do I really want to do this? Does it seem joyful? Is there something else I would rather do instead?" Take time to listen to your feelings. Do things only when they feel right and when you would love to do them; then you are operating from your wise will.

You can also develop your magnetic will. Magnetism is a powerful force. You can draw what you want to you by allowing it to come rather than by forcing it to come. When you push too hard to get things, you actually repel the things you are seeking. There is a different feeling between reaching out for something versus allowing it to come to you.

A great master creates by aligning with the Higher Will so that any action taken is "right" action. He or she then visualizes the desired result and becomes magnetic to that result. The master patiently waits for the right time to take action, and only takes action when it is appropriate to do so.

Think of something you have been wanting. Are you sending your will out, trying to force it to come? If so, you are working too hard. Instead, imagine that you are becoming magnetic to this thing. You may even want to pretend you are a magnet, drawing it to you. Create space in your energy and life for this thing to come in to. Open your heart to receive it. This way you are drawing things to you with your magnetic will rather than trying to make them come with force.

Receive energy from other people's hearts and not their centers of will.

Right use of will means learning not to let the forceful wills of others control you. There are several ways to know if other people are using their wills to manipulate you. One is through your mental or emotional resistance to them. Another is through an uncomfortable feeling in your body when you think of them, such as a pit in your stomach. If someone is trying to force you to do something, either subtly or not so subtly, you can work at an energy level to change things between you.

Start by getting quiet and thinking of the other person. As you think of this person, do you have an uncomfortable feeling anywhere in your body? Uncomfortable areas can indicate places where you have taken on other people's energies and are "wearing" their energy patterns rather than your own. Send light to this place, and imagine you are reclaiming your own energy in this area. Close off any area in which you have been receiving another's energy, and then add your own light to this area.

Pay attention to where other people are sending energies from as well, and only accept energies from their heart or higher centers. You can know if people are sending you energy from their will by getting quiet, thinking of them, and imagining you can tell if they have a "cord" of energy coming from their will center toward you. See yourself refusing this energy. Some people practice cutting cords, imagining that they "cut" the energy coming toward them from another person's will. The feeling that you are not accepting this energy is more important than the visualization you use. After you have "cut" this cord of energy, see it going back to them as energy they can use any way they want.

When you are with someone, practice sending energy through your heart. As you move all energy into your heart, you are evolving from operating from your center of will into living in your heart center as your Higher Self.

Offer assistance to others only when they ask for it.

As you become a source of light to others, your will can assist them in their growth, or it can interfere with their growth if you push too hard. Right use of your will means not using your forceful will on others. It means using your wise will when you work with people and not trying to make others change if they are not ready.

You can contribute to the desire to grow in your children, friends, and loved ones. Your wise will does things easily and gently, and takes action only when the timing is right. It waits until people are ready to hear what you have to say. When a friend comes to you and asks, "How can I learn what you have learned?" that is the time to assist him or her. Talking on and on about something to people who have not asked about it and are not interested in it may only turn them away.

If there is a quality you want your mate or a friend to have, demonstrate that quality yourself. As your life begins to work better you inspire others to discover the secrets you have found. Find more joy in your life, laugh more, and allow yourself to be happy.

One woman wished her husband would be more positive. In the past, she had tried to use her forceful will to change him, trying to make him change by pointing out often how negative he was. That only seemed to make him worse. Using her wise will, she decided to try increasing her own positiveness and stop pointing out how negative he was. She mentally told him she loved and accepted him just as he was. Slowly he became more positive without even realizing it. When she moved her will to her heart and became more loving, he was willing to grow and change.

You will be amazed at the power of one person focused on his own growth to transform the people he spends time with. One man went to work in an office where everyone, stressed and hurried, ate candy and unhealthy snacks all day. At first he found himself criticizing them, then he began eating the same kinds of food himself. One day, unhappy over his increasing lack of energy and rapid weight gain, he decided to start eating healthy food and brought interesting, healthy snacks with him every day. Soon, others were asking him about what he was eating. Over a period of several months many people in the office started eating healthier snacks. He never preached, criticized, or tried to get them to change. He taught them by example.

There is no one "right" way to grow. There are many paths to enlightenment and God. See what is beautiful in every person's path, in every religion, and in every belief system. Honor other people's paths even if they are different from yours. Be inclusive and loving, and look beyond the form of people's beliefs to the essence. There is no one right way; there is only the way that is right for you. There is something unique, perfect, and beautiful in every culture, in every system of belief. Look for what you have in common with others and accept and love those who are on different paths.

If you have been around people who wanted you to change a habit or do something differently, you know how their trying to get you to change made it harder to do. To create a desire to grow in others, share your enthusiasm about your life. Listen to people, draw them out, and find ways to assist them in loving themselves more. Grow yourself and become an example. Your great teachers, such as Buddha and Christ, came to earth to be examples of what you might become—a peaceful, loving, compassionate, and wise being.

R*ight* U*se of* W*ill*

MEDITATION

The purpose of this meditation is to learn how to use your will to achieve your higher purpose in the easiest, most joyful, loving, and gentle way.

Steps: Get into your Higher Self state for this meditation.

1. Imagine once again you can see your higher path stretching out in front of you all the way to the top of a mountain, as you did in the Linking With the Higher Will meditation on page 47. You are going to adjust your will to increase your ability to travel this path joyfully, easily, and wisely. As your Higher Self you can link directly with your will. Ask your will to work with you to assist you in traveling to the top of the mountain to reach your highest potential, accomplishing your goals of world service and spiritual growth in the easiest, most joyful way.

2. Go up this path now, imagining energy flowing from your heart into your will. This links your will with your heart. You now easily go toward that which you love, following the path of your heart. Picture everything that is not on the path of your heart falling away. The path that stretches in front of you up the mountain is now your heart's path, aligned with your will.

3. As you look up this path, think of how you normally use your will. How much energy or force normally do you use to get things done? Adjust this so that you are exerting just the right amount and letting yourself be carried

by the higher current as well as by your own will. How do other people affect your will? How is your will affected by your feelings? When you decide to do something, what things make it easier to take action and use your wise and loving will? How does your will become stronger? Ask your will how you could work with it to get things done in easier and higher ways.

4. See yourself going up this path with your will wisely leading you. Nothing stops you from going to the top. You are learning to use your will in the highest way, finding the higher current and flowing with it.

5. As you go up the path, you may need various tools. Imagine that your will is magnetic and that anytime you need something to accomplish your goals, you magnetize it to you. You simply send out a call for what you need and draw it right to you in the perfect time and in the perfect way.

6. Is there something in your life you have been wanting to do but feel you lack the willpower to do? Take a moment to ask your wise will why it isn't working with you toward this goal. Is there a better way to accomplish this goal, or is the goal the right one for you?

7. Continue all the way to the top. You are now at the top. Once again imagine your will linking with the Higher Will, so that you flow with the current and reach your highest evolution in this lifetime.

8. Come back into the room when you are ready, feeling a new sense of ease and joy as your wise and magnetic will is now operating with the Higher Will to bring you your goals and spiritual growth.

20

Non-Attachment

Developing the ability to let go will accelerate your growth. Think of a time in your life when you let go of something, when you made a change and things were even better than before. One of the challenges of spiritual growth is learning to release those things that no longer serve you, bless them as they leave, and embrace the new as it comes.

Letting go is an important aspect of growing. To grow, you may want to let go of an attitude, such as anger or sadness. Sometimes you will need to let go of roles, such as pretending to be a victim or savior. Sometimes you will need to let go of a relationship, a job, or a way of life. Learn to open to the new and release the old when it no longer serves you. Everything comes into your life to teach you something. When a person, situation, or thing has taught you all it can, your Higher Self will replace it with something that will offer you new opportunities to grow and evolve.

There is a common belief that growth requires suffering. One of the greatest causes of suffering is attachment. The more easily you can let go of the old and embrace the new, the more you can grow through joy rather than struggle. Growth involves making changes; learning new skills; and accepting new forms, attitudes, perspectives, and people into your life.

Some people think that they need to hang on to what they have, for it may be the best they will ever get. If you are thinking about making a change, imagine yourself having something even better than you have now. See yourself going through the process easily and feeling happy with the results. Imagine that this will be the best thing that has ever happened to you, even though you might not see why right now. Decide that you are going to trust in your ability to create your higher good, and look forward to the wonderful surprises that are in store for you.

Look at the things, people, and situations in your life right now. Is there anything that you would like to release? Ask your Higher Self to assist you in releasing anything that is not for your higher good. Is there anything that seems to be leaving your life even though you aren't sure you want it to? Take a deep breath, close your eyes, and mentally give this thing permission to leave you. Hanging on can repel something you want; once you release something, it will either come back to you or something better will take its place. Nothing ever leaves your life unless something better is coming.

Approach change as a great adventure. Believe that all change is for your higher good or it wouldn't be happening. You can learn to cope with change in joyful, peaceful ways by trusting that the universe is friendly and that your Higher Self loves you and is looking out for you. If your personality isn't willing to make the needed changes, sometimes your Higher Self will set things up so that the changes are made for you. Act upon the whispers before they become shouts; make the changes your inner self suggests to you.

One of the most difficult attachments to let go of might be your attachment to your viewpoint, beliefs, and judgments. You are always being challenged to think in new and expansive ways.

The path is easy
for those who have no preferences.

Let go of your strong preferences and opinions, for they are attachments that can take a lot of your energy. You can find your preferences in both significant and subtle things. Sometimes you have preferences in even the smallest things, such as the way your food is prepared or the way you drive to work every day. It is important to discover which preferences truly serve your higher good and which are simply unexamined habits that keep you from discovering new, higher ways to be.

Start practicing non-attachment by taking one small thing you feel attached to and pretending for one day that you are not attached to it. Become an observer and watch yourself. What habits and routines are you attached to? You don't have to give up these preferences, only your dependence on them. Once you can be happy with or without them you are free; you can have them in your life without being controlled by them.

You also need to learn detachment from strong emotions and situations that might take you out of your calm, clear center. You will want to let your Higher Self be the director of your consciousness. To do this, observe what is going on around you calmly and without judgment. It is as if you create an inner sanctuary, where only the guidance and direction of your Higher Self can influence you. As you stay aware and observant, you will be able to take action calmly.

Learn to trust your intuition and take action on the messages you receive. Sometimes you have something planned, and an inner voice encourages you to change your plans in some way. How quickly can you drop your attachment to following your original plans and make new ones? You will have increasing joy and ease when you listen to and immediately follow your inner messages.

To effectively get your work out to the world, you will need to learn to detach from what others think of you. It is important not to worry about being liked, appreciated, or understood. You are at the forefront of a new consciousness, and many of your ideas are new. It takes an evolved person to appreciate new ideas. Learn to detach from needing praise or validation; others may simply not be aware enough to see the value of what you are doing. Some people feel threatened by new ideas, and they may express skepticism or criticize your work. Learn to detach from people's reactions and value your work according to your own internal sense of its worth.

It is important to let go of personal ambition. If you are tuning in to and following the higher plan, all good things will come to you. Make your decisions not on what you think you will get out of doing things, but on how much your actions contribute to others. Although you still may have personal motives for what you do, make sure you are also considering the good of others.

Don't worry about the numbers of people who are drawn to your work. Simply follow your inner guidance and do the best job possible. It is better to reach one person who truly benefits from your work than a hundred who do not. You will be more empowered by the one who does than the hundred who do not.

Detach from needing to have things work out any certain way. The universe is perfect and there are no failures. You may seem to lose time, but in the grander scheme of things that time will always be made up for in other ways. Give yourself the gift of detaching from your worries and trust that everything is happening perfectly.

> N*on-attachment is serving*
> *people's Higher Selves*
> *rather than their personality selves.*

Some people confuse attachment with love. The thought of non-attachment worries them, for they think if they do not feel attached to people they do not love them. Non-attachment does not mean that you don't care; it is caring at a higher level. It is assisting them in being their Higher Selves rather than their personality selves.

Some of you worry that you feel less compassionate the more you grow. You may look at others and see that their suffering could be ended rapidly if they were willing to let go or make different decisions. Earlier, you may have felt sorry for them and thought that this was compassion. Compassion is remaining in your center, observing, and detaching emotionally from others' problems. It is looking at the highest thing you can do for them, not what their personalities are telling you they need.

Sometimes to assist people in higher ways you need to do things that feel right to you but may not feel comfortable to their personalities. For instance, you may need to tell your child she can't have something because you know having it might harm her. You are not attached to how her personality reacts, because you are serving her Higher Self. Non-attachment requires you to know what your values are, honor your truth, and come from your integrity so you can assist people at the highest level.

Attachment is wanting to take care of people and solve their problems for them. Non-attachment will give you a clearer perspective on how much assistance to give, how much people will be able to use your assistance, and when to stop giving to them. Sometimes the only thing you can do for people is simply love them and let them have their problems.

Learn to detach from people's personalities, pettiness, or little faults. Focus instead on their greatness and you will experience more of it. Non-attachment is loving people as they are and finding the right moment to insert a thought, a touch, or love into their lives to empower them to make a shift to a higher level of consciousness.

For instance, one woman suddenly got very busy with her work and was unable to spend her usual amount of time with a close friend. At first she felt guilty, for she knew her friend felt hurt. As she pondered how to love both herself and her friend, she detached from the personality needs of her friend and imagined talking directly to her friend's Higher Self. She asked what she could do to honor the Higher Self of her friend.

She received inner guidance to be with her friend during the most important times and not to worry about other times. She sensed that these times would be when her friend was getting ready to grow and shift her consciousness to a new level. She didn't know in advance when those times would be, but she spent time with her friend only when she felt drawn to be with her. As it so happened, those times ended up being significant turning points for each of them. Every time they were together, both of them had significant breakthroughs. By her serving her friend's Higher Self and not her personality, their friendship grew even stronger.

Some of you are attached to other people's opinions and base some of your actions and decisions on their love, approval, or validation. If you feel that you must be loved all the time and are afraid to do what you want because someone might stop loving you, your challenge will be to lose your attachment to needing that love. You may have a belief that says, "If I act like myself, if I ask for what I want, I won't be loved." Tell yourself that you can have what you want and that people love you for who you are. You are freer to be creative, grow, and fulfill your potential when you are not bound by what others think of you. Are the people you admire most the ones who always seek everyone's approval before they do things, or those who trust and act on their own inner messages?

You are not responsible for making other people's lives work; they are.

The need to save people from their mistakes is an attachment that will slow your growth. Are there people in your life you feel sorry for or are trying to bail out of problems they have created? You often turn into the "victim" when you try to save people, because they often end up blaming you for their problems. They might also try to make you feel bad if you withdraw your support or don't solve their problem. They may become dependent upon you and resent their dependency and your help. Your "help" may even cost you their friendship. There are times when it is important not to be attached to solving other people's problems.

You have the right not to hear about or become involved with other people's problems. Maintain a level of detached observation; decide if you can truly assist them and if they want or can even use your assistance. If you do decide to provide assistance to someone with a problem, make a conscious decision to do so.

When people tell you of their problems, stop and decide if you want to tackle their problems with them. Listen to them closely and decide if they are willing to find solutions, or if they simply want to complain about how bad the problem is. Decide how much time you are willing to commit to assisting people, and give them a clear picture of the time, energy, and resources you will commit to their problems.

Before you pour energy into changing or assisting people, let go of your need to have other people grow, appreciate you, or act in any particular way. Sometimes your strong desire to have them change may be the very thing that keeps them from growing. As you detach and stop worrying about them, they will be freer to grow.

We guides can give you much insight about your lives, but only you have the ability to change your life by using the advice. Sometimes you aren't ready to let go of your problems, because they are still teaching you many things. What we can do is assist you in gaining a new perspective, take a small step, or love yourself more. Do the same yourself; give other people what assistance you feel is best when viewing the situation from your highest level, then detach from the outcome.

As *you give freedom to others you become freer yourself.*

Over time people will come and go in your life, and one of the greatest gifts you give others is the freedom to go their own way. To truly serve others, you will need to give them complete freedom, for in so doing you also free yourself to be all you can be. Do not worry if some of your friends leave your life, for as you increase your vibration, people will either grow and stay in your life or leave.

Don't be hard on yourself if you don't feel like spending as much time as you used to with friends who refuse to grow. Be open to changes in them and encourage them when it is appropriate, but give yourself permission to spend your time where it brings you the most joy. You do not serve friends who aren't growing by staying at their level to keep them company and make them feel good. Only by growing yourself do you serve others.

You can invite these friends to "play" with you at your new, higher level. You are not sending them away. You are telling them you are playing a new, higher game and inviting them to play it with you. Release them with love and compassion if they do not want to play at your expanded level. It is more loving to release your friends than to put yourself around them and inwardly criticize their behavior.

For instance, you may have a friend who generally plays the victim and blames everyone in his life for his problems. You have decided to take responsibility for your life and make it work. You may wish that your friend would change and find yourself increasingly irritated at his behavior. Invite him to take responsibility for his life and play at your new level. Be willing to gently release him if he does not want to change, or you may find your energy being depleted when you are with him.

If your friends do leave your life, they may surprise you some day and come back, willing to play at a higher level with you. New friends will also come into your life who will match your higher vibration and new interests.

You will find much more joy and inner peace when you release your attachments. Your world will expand and new opportunities will present themselves. Developing the quality of non-attachment will give you freedom. When you aren't attached to what other people think of you or to having things be a certain way, you are free. You will have a sense of well-being no matter what the people around you are doing. Non-attachment is an important attitude on the path to spiritual mastery.

N*on-A*ttachment

MEDITATION

The purpose of this meditation is to let go of attachments to conditions, circumstances, people, and things that don't serve your higher path, and to attract to yourself those that do.

Steps: Get into your Higher Self state for this meditation.

1. Sit quietly, and imagine that at an energy level you are spinning, like a top or a star. Things are orbiting around you, attracted by the qualities and nature of your spin. These are the people, objects, and situations in your life right now. Get a sense of how fast you are spinning.

2. Now increase your spin to a speed that represents your next level of growth. Mentally picture your spin increasing to a higher, finer level. Your radiance is growing. As you continue to grow and increase your spin, you will eventually become pure, radiant light. Notice that as you increase your spin to the next level, some of the things orbiting around you are falling away, and new things are being attracted to you.

3. As a top or a star, become aware of lines of energy going out from you to everyone and everything in your life. These are all your connections and attachments. Move the center of the star and the lines of energy to your heart and make them even more radiant and beautiful. As you make them more beautiful you are creating a higher relationship to these things. Notice that as you send and receive

your energy connections through your heart center you increase your spin.

4. You are free to make the connections however you like, so explore and play with your new connections and spin. When you are ready, come back into the room and enjoy the newness of all you have chosen.

21

Becoming Transparent

As you put your work out to the world and grow through service, you will encounter many kinds of energies and people. You will become more aware of the subtle energies around you and of other people's thoughts and feelings. You will want to learn how to handle these energies in a way that allows you to be a source of light no matter what type of energy you are around.

Learning how to stay calm and centered in your own energy while experiencing the energies, thoughts, and feelings of the people around you might be called "being transparent." When you are transparent, you can comfortably be with many different kinds of people. You can learn to enjoy what is positive about them and find ways to go even higher when you are around energies that are not as harmonious as your own.

To grow spiritually, you do not need to create a perfect environment, have no negativity around you, or retreat from the world. You are here to learn how to be your Higher Self in the midst of the kinds of energies that are present on earth. You can grow and find love in your heart even around people who aren't of a similar vibration to you.

Some of you think that if you were truly an evolved being, you would have been born to parents who raised you in environments of total love and support. You think that you would already be fully evolved and perfect by now, never experiencing any pain or negativity. Instead, many of you wanted to be born into environments that would teach you about the energies in the world and help you become accustomed to them at an early age. You do not become strong by seeking those situations that keep you sheltered and protected; you become strong by learning to navigate all the different kinds of weather, finding your strength and direction from within. If you have felt any resentment because you had a difficult childhood, let go of it, and appreciate all the strength you gained from the situations you grew up with.

At various times in your life you may have been around people whom you had trouble loving. Look at the circumstances you have in your life right now. If you are around people or energies you aren't comfortable with, see them as offering you opportunities for spiritual growth by teaching you more about becoming transparent. The thoughts and feelings of people you have the most trouble harmonizing with are the very ones that will give you the most growth when you do learn to be transparent to them. That is why you have attracted these people into your life.

What kind of emotional energy do you find hardest to be peaceful around—anger, frustration, anxiety, impatience, hurt feelings, complaining, righteousness, stubbornness, indifference, incompetence, laziness, lack of self-direction, negativity, helplessness, neediness, manipulativeness, or controlling? Those are the very emotions you need to become increasingly transparent to in order to grow spiritually and gain more power. You could try to avoid these energies by changing jobs or moving away from neighbors who bother you. However, you will continually attract people with similar energies until you learn how to stay balanced and in your center around them.

To become transparent,
make no judgments about others' behavior.

To become transparent, start by not reacting to what people do. When you get emotional about their behavior you are not transparent to their energy. Once you are unemotional and acting from your calm, clear center, the actions you take will be the ones that create the most results.

One of the best ways to become transparent is to find some aspect of others' behaviors you can harmonize with. This will allow you to stay calm enough to know what action to take from a clear, balanced frame of mind. For instance, if a group is throwing a loud party next door and you find yourself getting angry, find something in their energy you like. You might tune in to the aspect of celebration, joy, and release that is present, even if it is expressed in a different form than you would use.

If someone is yelling at another person and you find yourself becoming upset, focus on the lessons the two are teaching each other, their caring, and their concern for the outcome. Within every situation there are higher and lower frequencies you can tune in to. You can become transparent to lower ones by not focusing on them but instead finding and tuning into the higher aspects of the situation.

If people are intimidating, threatening, or trying to control you, imagine them as one inch tall. Would you still respond in the same way? If people are angry or aggressive, see them as small children throwing tantrums, for they are expressing their little selves, not their Higher Selves.

If someone isn't behaving the way you want him to, send him love and acceptance for who he is rather than getting angry at him. You can practice this by visualizing yourself in a situation that bothered you in the past and imagining yourself responding with love. For instance, imagine yourself speaking to someone who is closed to you or drawing you into a power struggle. Fighting with him brings you down to his level. Instead, put light around yourself to make your own energy beautiful, open your heart, and refuse to allow his upset energy into your life. You can choose to let his emotions flow right through you as if they were made of a different frequency.

Sending love transforms the energy around you.

The vibration of your positive, loving thoughts will be finer than others' negativity, which will pass through you without striking a single chord. As your transparency increases, you will draw circumstances into your life that reflect your inner calm and peace, and you will rarely be near offensive or negative people. The more you can feel compassion for others and send them love, the more you will be transparent to their emotional states.

Awareness of other people's energies is a great gift. Your greater awareness lets you know when you need to be transparent. Before you walk into any place, take a moment to sense your own energy and then tune in to the energy of the place. Focus on the energy there that you can harmonize with. When you leave, check to see if your energy feels different from the way it felt earlier. If there is a difference, accept only the changes you choose. Knowing your own energy will give you a reference point and a way to know if you have let yourself be affected by the energies around you.

Many of you unconsciously "match" other people's energies when you are with them. You are probably very sensitive to the feelings of others and able to experience a wide range of feelings. The next time you are with people, notice if you are unconsciously matching their energies. If they are talking quickly does your breathing speed up? Do you begin talking faster yourself? If people are depressed, do you suppress your joyful feelings and join them? If people are angry, do you find yourself getting angry too? Start by watching your breathing, for you may be matching your breathing to theirs. It is partly the unconscious matching of breath that opens you to thoughts and energies you do not want. Breathe slowly and calmly. As you do, you will be more able to stay centered and calm.

People's feelings would not annoy you unless you had similar feelings, attitudes, or behaviors—however minor—yourself. Imagine that other people in your life are playing out roles to mirror back to you certain parts of yourself. When they act in ways you don't like, they are mirroring back to you a part of yourself that you haven't yet learned to love. As you learn to love and find the beauty in others, you will become transparent to their energies. You will also be sending love to the part of yourself that has similar feelings. As you learn to love every part of yourself, you will raise your vibration and no longer attract those kinds of people into your life.

Each time you raise the vibration of one of your emotions, you will no longer unconsciously take on the lower vibration of that emotion from another person. There will be no place in you that will attract that emotion from another. For instance, as you master your fear, you may recognize fear in others, but you won't feel their fear as if it were your own.

Learn to recognize when you have taken on other people's energies.

Some of you are such natural healers you unknowingly take on others' energies and need to become aware when you have done so. You may spend much time trying to make others' lives work, thinking of their problems and pain as your own. It takes a high degree of mastery to do this without lowering your own energy. Some of you unconsciously bring others' lower energies into yourself out of your great compassion and desire to assist them. When you are with people who are upset, you may start feeling upset yourself. They may go away feeling better, but you need to release the upset you took into yourself.

Learn to recognize when you have taken on others' energies and learn ways to release those energies. Others' energies won't feel different from your own—they will exaggerate and amplify your own feelings. If after being with someone you are feeling sad, angry, or some other feeling that is unusual for you or stronger than normal, you may have brought other people's feelings and emotions into yourself.

If you have taken on energy that is not your own, there are ways to release it. Just realizing that you are not feeling the way you were feeling before you saw the person can help release that person's energy. At a physical level, you can remove the energy of others from your body through deep breathing, yoga, exercise, and bodywork. Stopping from time to time throughout the day and taking several deep breaths will assist you in clearing your energy. Some of you release energy by getting angry or having an outburst of crying or laughter. As you increase your vibration you will no longer have pent-up emotions from taking in others' feelings; you will be able to see the energy patterns in your aura that are not yours and release them with your mental command.

As you go higher, you may choose to transmute energy rather than become transparent to it. At a high degree of mastery, you may knowingly take on some of other people's denser, less harmonized energies so you can assist them in transmuting and releasing them. Your great masters are willing to take on others' negativity and transmute it into a higher frequency of positive energy and love that they then send back. Until you gain a great skill at doing this, it is better to simply become transparent to others' energies rather than to try to take it into yourself and change it.

Many of you live in cities and are around the energy fields of many people. This creates a vast array of emotional energies that can influence you. These emotional energies move in vortexes, as similar emotions attract each other and move through large areas as a mass of energy. Such a mass can be compared to a weather front moving through your physical dimension. As you become calmer and more transparent, you are less affected when you are in these energies.

You can know if you are letting these energies affect you by becoming more observant of your thoughts and emotions. Are you feeling fine one moment and depressed, sad, or anxious the next with no apparent reason for the change? Do you feel sluggish all day and discover when talking to your friends that they have been feeling the same way for no reason? The energy exercise at the end of this chapter can assist you in becoming transparent to these energies or any negative energies that you do not wish to experience.

The emotional energies of large groups of people create what can be seen as "weather" on other planes of reality as well as your own. Sometimes when you have trouble meditating, channeling, or being creative, you may actually be experiencing "astral storms" that can make it more difficult to reach upward. The astral dimension is vibrating at a slightly different frequency from your universe and is composed mostly of emotional energy. It has many levels. At its lower levels are the dense, negative emotions, and at its higher levels are the emotions of bliss and ecstasy.

When you are experiencing joyful, happy feelings, you vibrate with the higher levels of the astral plane and actually dissolve many of your less harmonious emotions. You do not need to dwell on your negative emotions to dissolve them, for every minute you spend feeling calm and peaceful increases your vibration and begins to release your less harmonious emotions.

*You have the ability to feel
the way you want
at all times.*

You can feel peaceful, calm, centered, and balanced no matter who is around or what is happening. As you learn to become transparent, you will find your sensitivity increasing, for there is great advantage in being able to sense energy at an increasingly refined level. Your sensitivity is a gift—it allows you to discern what is going on around you with greater accuracy, decide your course of action, and move forward with fuller awareness of the circumstances and possibilities. Your calm and peace will be a gift to others and make a contribution to shifting their awareness to a higher consciousness.

Becoming Transparent

MEDITATION

X

The purpose of this meditation is to become transparent and let people's energies pass through without affecting you.

You can use this technique anytime you are around energy you don't like. You can do this meditation when you are alone or with other people. If you have a friend present, you may want to sit with this person and let him or her sense your energy while you are practicing becoming transparent. Often people can feel a difference at the moment you become transparent, and their feedback is valuable. Observe as much as you can about what you can do to enhance the effect of being transparent.

Steps: Get into your Higher Self state for this meditation.

1. Breath deeply and relax your body. Call light to you and put a cocoon of light all around you. Bring this light very close to your body. It will feel powerful and intense; you are compacting this light into an area about one inch away from your body all around you. It will look like an outline of radiant light all around your body.

2. Begin to withdraw your energy from inside this layer of light, imagining you are putting it into another dimension or frequency, until this light is surrounding a void. As you remove your energy, imagine others' energies passing right through this void. You are now transparent. Play with how long you can keep your energy in another frequency and how it feels as you do.

3. As you put your energy back inside the cocoon of light, notice how much lighter and more harmonious your energy has become.

4. You may also want to imagine sending love to the other person or people around you if you are around energy you want to be transparent to, for as you send love you will not pick up others' energies.

5. When you are ready, return to the room, feeling fully yourself.

Epilogue:
The Vision

Love every part of your process of spiritual growth. Some days you will embrace all your new ideas about how you might live your life, and other days you might not want to think about them. Sometimes you will be doing much inner work, and at other times you will be making many changes in your outer life.

Everything goes in cycles, including your spiritual growth. Some cycles are yearly, some weekly. There are longer growth cycles as well, such as seven-year cycles, with one activity or a certain pace and rhythm being prominent during that time. One cycle may be a retreat from the world, and another may be an outward thrust. You may have monthly or yearly cycles of intense spiritual realizations followed by periods of quiet activity, integration, and emotional growth. The intensity of your focus on growth ebbs and flows as you open to new realizations and then integrate them with the rest of your life.

You *don't need to change yourself; you only need to love yourself.*

Your Higher Self is leading you to all the things you need to do to grow spiritually. It is always there, guiding and loving you. You have all the answers within you. Spiritual growth is an individual path. It is important to follow your own inner wisdom about what to do and when to do it. Realize that whatever you are doing right now is perfect for you. Stop *trying* to be perfect. Everything you are doing is *already* perfect. Let go of any judgments you may have about how evolved you are or what you ought to be doing to grow spiritually. Start by loving where you are right now in your growth.

As you grow spiritually, you move into higher and higher levels of consciousness. What is life like at these higher levels? You have released old programming and beliefs that no longer serve you. You have drawn into your life supportive, positive people. You empower yourself and others in all you do and say. You know who you are, why you are here, and what your higher purpose is. Your life-style and environment support your life purpose and greater work in the world. You explore new possibilities and choices and continually expand your vision of what is possible. You have the tools to draw to yourself the opportunities, people, and events you need to create your life's work. You operate from your heart, and you trust your inner messages and take action upon them.

You are conscious of the energy around you, deciding when to be transparent to it, harmonize with it, or transmute it to a higher order.

You are aware of your energy and the effects other people have upon it. You are present in the moment—alert, aware, and at a high level of observation all the time. Your increasing aliveness, enthusiasm, and growth spark growth in everyone around you.

As your Higher Self, you create with energy before you take physical action. You know you can create whatever you want by working with the higher forces and directing your thoughts, emotions, and intent toward your goals. You create change by working at the highest spiritual level rather than working at the personality level. You stop before you take action, go within, and receive guidance from your Higher Self about what action to take. As you grow, you know that anything is possible. You know that through your understanding of how energy works you can consciously create what seemed like miracles when you had less understanding of the way energy works.

You are able to create what you want at a speed that seemed impossible at earlier levels of growth. You are able to handle easily and joyfully the things that used to challenge you. Your lessons may come faster, but you will also have the tools to move through them more quickly and easily.

The rewards of spiritual growth are many—a clearer sense of direction, a greater feeling of being in control, and a deeper understanding of why things are happening. There is an increasing calm that comes as you begin to enjoy and understand your life. You can truly live a life than is joyful and loving to yourself.

Relax for a moment and take a deep breath. Call light to yourself and surround yourself with light. Put your hand over your heart and tell yourself you love and accept yourself just as you are. Spend a moment acknowledging how far you have already come. Affirm your commitment to your higher purpose and world service. Feel the higher community of beings you are a part of sending you love and support. Merge completely with your Higher Self; you and your Higher Self are now one. Allow the love of your Higher Self to penetrate every cell in your body and show you your divinity.

Take a moment before you put this book down and ask yourself what one step you could take right now that would contribute the most to your spiritual growth. Then, take it!

Companion Books for Spiritual Growth

Orin books:

BOOK I OF THE EARTH LIFE SERIES

Living with Joy
Keys to Personal Power and Spiritual Transformation

This book teaches you how to love and nurture yourself, live in higher purpose, and discover your life purpose. You will learn how to radiate love; be compassionate, tolerant, and forgiving; feel inner peace; take a quantum leap; gain clarity; open to new things; trust your inner guidance; change negatives into positives; and open to receive. You will learn to raise your vibration by increasing your ability to love; have more self-esteem; and create harmony, clarity, and peace around you. You can live with joy rather than struggle.

BOOK II OF THE EARTH LIFE SERIES

Personal Power Through Awareness
A Guidebook for Sensitive People

This is an accelerated, step-by-step course in sensing energy. Using these easy-to-follow processes, thousands have learned to create immediate and profound changes in their relationships, self-image, and ablity to love and be loved. You need no longer be affected by other people's moods or negativity. You can recognize when you have taken on other people's energies and easily release them. You can learn to stay centered and balanced, know who you are, increase the positive energy around you, and help and heal others. Your sensitivity is a gift. Learn to use it to send and receive telepathic messages, increase your intuitive abilities, and open to higher guidance. You can leave the denser energies, where things are often painful, and live in the higher energies where you can feel more loving, calm, focused, and positive.

Orin and DaBen books:

Opening to Channel
How to Connect With Your Guide
By Sanaya Roman and Duane Packer
As you develop your awareness of the inner planes of reality, you may want to connect with and verbally channel a high-level guide to assist you with your spiritual growth. Channeling is a skill that can be learned, and Sanaya and Duane, with their guides Orin and DaBen, have successfully trained thousands to channel using these safe, simple, and effective processes. You will learn how to tell if you are ready, how to attract a high-level guide, and how to go into trance. You can learn to channel to bring through knowledge, personal and spiritual guidance, healing techniques, and more.

Creating Money
Keys to Abundance
By Sanaya Roman and Duane Packer
This step-by-step guide to creating money and abundance was given to Sanaya and Duane by their guides Orin and DaBen. Thousands have manifested prosperity and created their life's

work using the simple processes contained in this book. Learn the spiritual laws of abundance, advanced manifesting techniques, and how to discover and draw to yourself your life's work. Learn about magnetism and how to use your magnetic will to draw to you what you want effortlessly, including the people you can serve and assist and the tools you need to carry out your life's work. Develop unlimited thinking, listen to your inner guidance, and transform your beliefs. Create money as a source of light for yourself and others. You can work with energy to easily create what you want and tap into the unlimited abundance of the universe.

More From Orin

Audio Cassette Tapes

"I offer you these processes as a way to grow with joy and ease. These guided journeys will help you relax, connect with your inner wisdom, release subconscious programs that aren't bringing you what you want, and replace them with higher, more positive ones. You will bring in the power of your soul, raise your vibration, and connect with the higher dimensions. You will be able to see immediate results in your life as you open to your greater potential."

– Orin

Spiritual Growth Tape Albums

Spiritual Growth tape albums (SG101 and SG102) contain inaudible sound frequencies which synchronize your brain waves to a theta state and harmonize the brain waves on both sides of your brain. When listened to with stereo headphones, these tapes will help you reach deep meditation in minutes. Theta is the state you experience right before you fall asleep, and it allows you to access memories, visualize, become more intuitive, receive insights, develop clairvoyance, inspiration, and expanded thinking. Both sides of your brain working together allows access to your higher abstract mind where information is processed and understood instantly.

Spiritual Growth: Volume I – Raising Your Vibration

Guided meditations for: Choosing Your Reality, Raising Your Vibration, Expanding and Contracting Time, Accelerating Your Growth, Right Use of Will, Lifting the Veils of Illusion, Becoming Transparent, and Calming Your Emotions. 4 tapes, 8 processes in cassette album. (SG101) $59.95 ** *(Tapes not sold separately)*

Spiritual Growth: Volume II – Being Your Higher Self

Guided meditations for: Connecting with the Universal Mind, Linking with the Higher Will, Being Your Higher Self, Creating with Light, Seeing the Bigger Picture, Non-Attachment, Allowing Your Higher Good, Opening Awareness of the Inner Planes. 4 tapes, 8 processes in cassette album. (SG102) $59.95 ** *(Tapes not sold separately)*

** Buy both Volumes I and II at the same time for $99.95 and save $19.95. Specify SG103. *(Free tape offer does not apply)*

Additional Resources

Guided Meditations by Orin

Spiritual Growth Affirmations Side 1, Guided Journey Side 2. Based on principles in book (SG100).
Living With Joy Affirmations and Guided Journey (L100)
Personal Power Through Awareness Affirmations, Guided Journey (P100)
Creating Money Affirmations, Magnetism exercises (M001)
Meeting Your Spirit Guides (014)
Who Am I? (017)
Self-Love (L102)
Radiating Unconditional Love (P103)
Opening Spiritually (SG002)
I Am Lovable (SI105)
Traveling into Probable Realities (SI018)
Developing Telepathy (015)
Feeling Inner Peace (L101)
Trusting Your Inner Guidance (SI107)
Staying In Your Center (SG003)
Unlimited Thinking (SI108)
Developing Intuition (010)
Developing Compassion/Forgiveness (SI104)
Discovering Your Life Purpose (L104)
The Universe is Perfect, Stop Efforting (SG004)
Opening Up Your Psychic Abilities (013)
Age Regression (SI041)
Past-Life Regression (SI043)
Creating Your Perfect Day (SI101)
Lucid Dreaming–Interpreting, Remembering Dreams (SI024)
Opening Creativity (SI046)
Opening to Receive (L106)
Clearing Blockages (SI057)
Taking a Quantum Leap (L103)
Attracting Your Soul-Mate (RE002)
Attunement With Your Crystal by Orin and DaBen (OD001) $12.50
(These tapes do not contain theta sound frequencies)

All tapes listed above are $9.98 each unless otherwise indicated. Include postage as per order form; CA residents add sales tax. For information on additional tapes from Orin, write address below.

To receive a FREE SUBSCRIPTION to our newsletter with information from Orin and DaBen on current earth changes, articles of interest, tape programs, and seminars by Orin and DaBen write or call: LuminEssence Productions, P.O. Box 19117, Oakland, CA 94619 (415) 635-1246

Be sure to include your name, address and phone number.

Audio Cassette Tape Albums

Learn to Channel

A set of four tapes containing over 16 processes by Orin and DaBen to help you open to channel. To be used with the book *Opening to Channel*. Included: Relaxation, Focus and Concentration Techniques; Journey to the Higher Realms to prepare you for your opening; Trance Posture; Opening to verbally channel; Questions to ask your Guide in trance; Instructions to give yourself a reading; and learn how to give readings to other people. Set of 4 tapes containing over 16 processes in vinyl album. (C100) $49.95 *(Free tape offer does not apply)*

Creating Money: Keys to Abundance

To increase your prosperity consciousness, Orin has made these Creating Money audio cassette tapes. These tapes are guided meditations that will assist you in reprogramming your subconscious to increase your abundance potential. The tapes in this series are:

Magnetizing Yourself (SI010)
Clearing Beliefs and Old Programs (SI071)
Releasing Doubts and Fears (SI075)
Linking with Your Soul and the Guides (SI076)
Aura Clearing, Energy, and Lightwork (SI073)
Subpersonality Journey: Awakening Your Prosperity Self (SI074)
Success: Releasing Fears of Success, Failure, Going for It! (SI070)
Abundance: Creating Plenty in EVERY Area of Your Life (SI072)

All tapes are $9.98 each. A complete set of all 8 processes as listed above is available in the Creating Money album (M100) for $49.95. The set contains 4 two-sided tapes packaged in a convenient cassette album. Please add postage and tax as per order form. *(Free tape offer does not apply to M100)*

Abundance Affirmation Cards

Affirmations from the book *Creating Money*. 112 Affirmations on quality blue-linen calling cards, shrink-wrapped in box. Pull one for your daily abundance affirmation. (CMA) $7.95

Abundance Crystal

Clear quartz crystal charged by Orin to assist you in creating abundance as you hold it. (CRY01) $7.95

Other Crystals Charged by Orin

Orin has personally held and charged each crystal with certain energies to assist you with your spiritual growth. As you hold them, they will help amplify your own energy.

Amethyst crystal: Orin has added some of the higher frequencies of his dimensions to assist you in being your Higher Self. (CRY03) $7.95

Citrine crystal: Hold this as you reprogram and add light at a cellular level and release old patterns. (CRY02) $7.95

Rose Quartz: Orin has charged these with love to assist you in loving yourself and opening your heart. (CRY06) $7.95

Clear Quartz crystal: Charged by Orin to assist you in traveling and exploring the higher dimensions and inner planes of reality. Can also be used to enhance telepathic sending and receiving. (CRY05) $7.95

Books

Living with Joy, by Sanaya Roman, channel for Orin. Keys to Personal Power and Spiritual Transformation. (H J Kramer Inc, 1986, 216 pages.) (LWJ) $9.95

Personal Power Through Awareness, by Sanaya Roman, channel for Orin. A Guidebook for Sensitive People (H J Kramer Inc, 1989, 216 pages) (PPTA) $9.95

Opening to Channel: How to Connect With Your Guide by Sanaya Roman and Duane Packer, channels for Orin and DaBen. (H J Kramer Inc, 1987, 264 pages) (OTC) $12.95

Creating Money: Keys to Abundance, by Sanaya Roman and Duane Packer, channels for Orin and DaBen. (H J Kramer Inc, 1988, 288 pages) (CM) $12.95

Seminars and Courses

Orin and DaBen give several weekend seminars and intensive throughout the year in the San Francisco Bay Area. Seminars include meditations, energy work, and channeling by Orin and DaBen. You will have opportunities to ask personal questions of Orin and DaBen, and they will teach you many techniques to assist you in experiencing higher states of consciousness. Write for information on dates and topics.

LuminEssence Productions • P.O. Box 19117 • Oakland, CA 94619
(415) 635-1246

Order Form

BUY ANY THREE TAPES FOR $9.98
GET A FOURTH $9.98 TAPE FREE!!
(Free tape offer does not apply to tape albums.)

Your Name _____

Address _____

City _____ State _____ Zip _____

Telephone: Home (_____) _____ Work (_____) _____
(In case we have any questions about your order.)

QTY	ITEM	DESCRIPTION	PRICE

POSTAGE RATES:

	First Class Mail*	U.P.S.
Up to $12 ...	$1.45	$2.00
$13 to $25 ...	$2.50	$2.50
$26 to $45 ...	$4.25	$3.00
$46 to 65 ...	$5.75	$3.75
$66 to $85 ...	$7.25	$4.50
$86 to $100 ...	$8.00	$5.75
Over $100 ...	$10.00	$7.00

*For First Class shipping of books
add .50 for each book ordered.*

Subtotal	
Sales tax*	
Postage	
Priority handling ($3.00)	
TOTAL	

*CA residents add
appropriate sales tax.

☐ Check here if you prefer your order shipped UPS.
(UPS cannot deliver to PO Box addresses.)

Payment enclosed: ☐ Check ☐ Money Order
Please charge my: ☐ VISA ☐ MasterCard

*Thank You
for
Your Order!*

Credit Card No. _____ Exp. Date _____

Signature as on card _____

Please make check payable to **LuminEssence Productions**. Canadian and foreign orders payable in U.S. Funds. Canadian and Mexican orders add $2.00 to U.S. Postage; other foreign orders add $7.50 to U.S. Postage. All orders will be shipped surface rate unless special air fee arrangements are made. Regular orders will be shipped within 2 weeks of receipt; priority-handling orders will be shipped within 72 hours of receipt. Remember to allow time for U.S. Mail or UPS delivery after order is shipped. Incomplete orders will be returned.   G1

COMPATIBLE BOOKS FROM H J KRAMER INC

WAY OF THE PEACEFUL WARRIOR
by
Dan Millman
*A story of mystery and adventure ideally suited to empower your
transformative process.
Available in book and audio cassette format*

TALKING WITH NATURE
by
Michael J. Roads
*A guidebook to help you align with the energies
of the plant and animal kingdoms.*

EAT FOR HEALTH
by
William Manahan, M.D.
*A loving and compassionate book that will help you
change your eating habits.*

SEEDS OF LIGHT
by
Peter Rengel
*A book of poetry on varied subjects to help align you
with your higher self.*

JOY IN A WOOLLY COAT
by
Julie Adams Church
*A book that reminds us of our interdependence with
the animal kingdom while it provides grief support
for pet loss.*

BIOCIRCUITS
by
Leslie Patten with Terry Patten
*A simple technology ideally suited for home use, biocircuits will provide you
with a direct experience of life force energy.*

SINGING MAN
by
Neil Anderson
*An allegorical tale of transformation. ''It is a true story, for on some
level it is happening to each of us now.''*—Jean Houston